INVEST YOUR FUTURE

INVEST YOUR FUTURE

Making godly choices using your head,
your heart and your Bible

Paul Mallard

INTER-VARSITY PRESS
36 Causton Street, London SW1P 4ST, England
Email: ivp@ivpbooks.com
Website: www.ivpbooks.com

First published 2022

British Library Cataloguing-in-Publication Data
A catalogue record for this book is available from the British Library.

ISBN: 978–1–78974–358–6
eBook ISBN: 978–1–78974–359–3

Set in Minion Pro 11/14pt
Typeset in Great Britain by CRB Associates, Potterhanworth, Lincolnshire
Printed and bound in Great Britain by Ashford Colour Press Ltd.

Produced on paper from sustainable sources

*Inter-Varsity Press publishes Christian books that are true to the Bible and that communicate
the gospel, develop discipleship and strengthen the church for its mission in the world.*

*IVP originated within the Inter-Varsity Fellowship, now the Universities and Colleges Christian
Fellowship, a student movement connecting Christian Unions in universities and colleges
throughout Great Britain, and a member movement of the International Fellowship
of Evangelical Students. Website: www.uccf.org.uk. That historic association is maintained,
and all senior IVP staff and committee members subscribe to the UCCF Basis of Faith.*

To Bruce and Allison, Clover and Melissa:
thank you for your fellowship spanning forty years of ministry.
The Lord is good and his mercy endures for ever.

Contents

Introduction

Trust in the Lord

Len Moss was born on 24 September 1921.

It was during the writing of this book that Len celebrated his centenary.

Len wasn't able to attend church but recorded a video which we played during our morning service.

With the sound of his great-grandchildren in the background, Len thanked God for his goodness and faithfulness over his long life. He had walked with his Saviour for nearly eighty years and wanted us to rejoice with him.

In a clear voice full of conviction Len looked into the camera and encouraged us to trust our lives to God: 'I want to celebrate what the Lord has done for me. Great is the Lord and greatly to be praised. It is good to trust in the Lord.'

Len concluded by quoting Solomon's wise and much-loved words,

Trust in the Lord with all your heart
 and lean not on your own understanding;
in all your ways submit to him,
 and he will make your paths straight.
(Prov. 3:5–6)

Looking back over a century of experience, Len had learned the great secret of guidance – God has promised to guide and we are called to follow.

Proverbs 3:5–6 encourages us to take God as our Guide and to walk with him in humble and confident faith. Trusting God will mean that we will obey his commands because we believe he knows what is best. It will help us to wait for his direction even if the way is hard and he seems to be silent. It means that we will not hold back from stepping out in faith when the way seems clear. It means that we will not try to twist the Bible when it points us in a direction we do not want to go. It means knowing that if God did not spare his Son but gave him up for us all, he will also, along with him, graciously give us all things (Rom. 8:32). Like William Carey, whose motto was, 'Expect great things from God. Attempt great things for God,'[1] we will be confident about the journey.

Len would agree.[*]

Finding the way

I began my pastoral ministry in January 1982.

From the outset I conducted a weekly surgery. This gave people the opportunity to come and ask questions and seek counsel. It was a fascinating experience. I continued the practice for the best part of thirty-five years; three or four hours a week, forty-five weeks a year.

People asked all sorts of question. Some were troubled by an obscure doctrine, while others struggled with discipleship. They shared their fears and their hopes, their battles and their burdens. Some just needed an arm around the shoulder and a word of encouragement.

As I look back, one subject dominated – the desire to know God's will. The request came in a variety of forms and in a multiplicity of situations. For some it was a cool and almost theoretical enquiry. For others it was a pressing need that had life-changing consequences. But in every case, there was a longing to know God's will and to please him.

People are fascinated by the subject of guidance. I have discovered more than thirty-five books that address it. (You may well be asking, why write another one?!)

---

[*] We will return to Solomon's words later in this book.

Why?

So why a book on guidance?

The first reason is that it fascinates Christians and they yearn to know the will of God. Life is full of choices. Most of them are of minor importance, but some have massive consequences. There is nothing more important than pleasing God. Surely there is no higher motivation than this. If we seek to live according to God's will, we can expect to experience his blessing. As we shall see, there is no guarantee of a comfortable life for those who live their lives in conformity to God's will, but there are clear promises of his smile and of his grace extended to us. Life is complicated. We want to get it right. This is a vital aspect of our everyday lives.

The second reason is fear. What if I get it wrong? There is a common and disconcerting idea that if I somehow misread the signs and fail to grasp God's plan, I may end up sidelined. God's perfect plan for my life will remain unrealized. I will never quite fulfil the potential God had for me. The angst that this generates can be paralysing for some of us. The fear of making the wrong decision leaves us unwilling to make any decision. In effect, we decide not to decide. God has a perfect plan for my life – what if I miss it?

A third reason for wrestling with this subject is the confusion that often surrounds it. We become angry with God because he does not make it easy for us. How do we find guidance? Guidance is about using the Bible and using our mind. Is it that simple? People make so many suggestions that it can be bewildering. Should I lay out a fleece like Gideon?† He is commended as a man of faith in Hebrews 11:32. Should we follow his example? What about the principle of the open door? When do I know if the door is open? What about strong impressions or words of knowledge or helpful advice? Where does wisdom come into it?

But there is a fourth reason why this subject is important. I guess that this has dawned on me over the years as I have tried to help people to discern the will of God. The biggest challenge is not finding

---

† The story of Gideon's fleece is found in Judges 6:33–40 and is often cited as a model for seeking guidance. We will return to him later!

3

'God's plan', but knowing God. This is because the purpose of my life is to know God and to glorify him forever. In his book *Knowing God*, Jim Packer puts it like this: 'Once you become aware that the main business that you are here for is to know God, most of life's problems fall into place of their own accord.'[2]

The process of guidance may sometimes seem torturous. We may be filled with doubts and anxieties. As we look back, we may regret some of our decisions and lament our lack of wisdom. However, the most important thing about our spiritual journey is not the route that we take but the Guide whom we follow. On this journey we are supposed to come to know and trust God. Through the process of guidance, we are supposed to see God.

After the Israelites' sin with the golden calf, God promised that he would go ahead of his people and guide them so that they would still inherit the promised land. However, he went on to declare, 'Go up to the land flowing with milk and honey. But I will not go with you, because you are a stiff-necked people, and I might destroy you on the way' (Exod. 33:3).

The people responded with lamentation: 'When the people heard these distressing words, they began to mourn and no one put on any ornaments' (Exod. 33:4).

What is the point of having the gifts without the Giver? What is the point of knowing guidance without enjoying fellowship with the Guide?

Structure

After a preliminary chapter in which we will try to clear away some common misunderstandings about guidance, this book is divided into three parts.

In Part 1 we will explore the main principles of guidance. How does God guide us? What is the role of the Bible and sanctified common sense? What about the Holy Spirit? Should we consider other forms of guidance – strong impressions, circumstantial pointers, the wisdom of friends? We will conclude by suggesting seven steps we might take as we seek to make wise decisions.

In Part 2 we will begin to apply these principles. The will of God encompasses every area of our lives – if my life is a many-roomed mansion, there can be no locked doors. Most daily decisions are comparatively straightforward and of minor significance. But some decisions have long-term consequences. They cluster around three subjects:

- Church: How do I find the right church?
- Work: How can I find the right job?
- Marriage: Should I get married, and if so, to whom?

In Part 3 we will address the bigger question of how God may be using the process of guidance to help us to grow towards maturity as disciples of Jesus Christ. How does he use this process to draw us into a deeper relationship with him? How does the process challenge our presuppositions and priorities? What does God want us to learn?

The goal of this book is to help us to think through the principles of guidance so that we can make decisions that are pleasing to God. But it also aims to do more than this. We need to increase our confidence in God so that we can rest in the knowledge that, however hard the way may be, it is well with our soul and that in all things God is working for our good.

> We can walk without fear, full of hope and courage and strength to do His will, waiting for the endless good which He is always giving as fast as He can get us able to take it in.[3]

1

Clearing the decks

Stranded in Boston

In 1990, my family had a really big adventure.

Most of our holidays were spent somewhere in the south of England or in the beautifully rugged landscape of Wales. But in 1990 we went to Florida.

I was booked to visit a church in Detroit, and we decided that we would take our three children with us and spend a week at Walt Disney World. The children had never flown before and the prospect of visiting the land where their favourite G. I. Joes were located filled my two boys with delight. Our daughter, who was three, just wanted to experience the Teacup ride at Disney.

I explained all this to the tour operator who was arranging the flights. I had never taken my family on such a trip, and he must have picked up my anxiety. Smiling, he said soothingly, 'It will be easy. You only have to change once – in Boston. You will have at least half an hour. Just make sure you make the connection. You don't want to be stranded for three weeks in Boston!'

I thought no more about it till the night before the journey.

To catch an 8 am flight we had to leave home at 3 am. We went to bed early, but I kept watching the clock in a kind of delirium of half-sleep. The phrase 'stranded in Boston' kept coming into my mind. In the dark hours we are often haunted by unfounded fears.

As it turned out, the flight from Heathrow landed ahead of time and we made our connection comfortably, and I look back with embarrassment in even telling the story.

Yet that is often the way in which we think about guidance.

Deciding not to decide

We think of the plan for our lives as a kind of complicated itinerary drawn up for us by a divine travel agent. We call it 'the will of God'. It is unique for every one of us. God may have given us general guidelines in the Bible, but this is different. It has not been revealed, but it clearly exists. It is the ideal blueprint for our lives, which God has designed. Like the journey to Florida, there are certain places that we have to be in order to make the connection. If we miss the first connection, we will never complete the journey. We have to be in the right place at the right time. But what if we go to the wrong place? What happens if we miss a connection? We may be able to revise the plan and catch up. Or we might just get stranded. Worst-case scenario – we will end up stranded in Boston.

On this view, my responsibility is twofold: somehow I have to discover the plan, and then I have to follow it.

Discovering God's perfect plan does involve making choices. If I am faced with two choices, either of which could be correct, how do I discover which one is God's ideal plan for my life? Depending on my experience or church background, this may involve special revelations, dreams, fleeces, the direction of a spiritual counsellor, meditation on the Bible or some combination of the above. Given enough patience and time I can discover what God wants. Then I just have to do it – that is the easy part!

But what if I get it wrong? What if I misunderstand God's plan and take the wrong path? What if I join the wrong church or marry the wrong person or start on the wrong career path? God will not desert me, but I will be doomed to experience his second best for my life. I will be stranded in Boston!

If God's plan for our lives is a complicated series of decisions and we are responsible for reading them right and never going astray, then it is possible to miss God's best and end up with his second- or third-best plan for our lives. In spiritual terms, I will end up on the scrapheap. I will have lost my usefulness to God.

So how do we respond to this? If this is our view of guidance, then we may make the decision not to decide! It can paralyse our thinking and prevent us from taking steps of faith just in case we get it wrong. We are so risk averse that we do not attempt anything of any significance, just in case.

We are like the man in the parable of the talents. Entrusted with treasures by his master he responds with fear:

> Then the man who had received one bag of gold came. 'Master,' he said, 'I knew that you are a hard man, harvesting where you have not sown and gathering where you have not scattered seed. So I was afraid and went out and hid your gold in the ground. See, here is what belongs to you.'
> (Matt. 25:24–25)

We might think that is the way of prudence and wisdom. The Master does not agree!

> His master replied, 'You wicked, lazy servant! So, you knew that I harvest where I have not sown and gather where I have not scattered seed? Well then, you should have put my money on deposit with the bankers, so that when I returned I would have received it back with interest.'
> (Matt. 25:26–27)

The fear of making mistakes can paralyse our thinking and keep us from obedience.

In the Bible we are called to bold and courageous faith which steps out and trusts that God will not let us down. We are not called to face the future with anxiety and apprehension.

A better way

The problem with this view is that it is based on a defective understanding of both the character of God and the nature and purpose of guidance.

It assumes that God is subject to our will and that, if we make a mistake, he does not have the wisdom or ability to get us back on track. We may even fear that he will give up on us and write us off.

It is possible to make dire mistakes that have unavoidable consequences. If I deliberately break my marriage covenant, I may know forgiveness and a restoration of the marriage relationship; however, I might find that some avenues of ministry are now closed to me. David's sin was forgiven, but there were consequences for him and for his family, which persisted (2 Sam. 12:11–14).

But even in the case of deliberate sin, God can overrule the consequences and turn all things to good. That is what he did in the story of Joseph and his brothers (Gen. 50:20), and supremely at Calvary (Acts 2:22–24). Human sin cannot frustrate God's purpose.

Of course, foolish decisions can have long-term consequences. But the idea that our mistakes can frustrate God's purposes involves a caricature of God that is utterly unworthy of him. It makes him a helpless observer who is unable to overrule the foolish decisions of his children. It doubts his wisdom, goodness and power. He is the one who is able to restore the locust-eaten years (Joel 2:25).

The Bible is full of people who made mistakes and were restored. Some of these mistakes may have been errors of judgment. Others were acts of sinful disobedience. Abraham pimped his wife, Moses murdered an Egyptian, David sinned with Bathsheba, Peter denied the Lord. None of these things made them irredeemably second-class. God is the God of grace who is in the business of restoring failures. If he could restore these people who had sinned grievously, is he not able to restore us when we make an honest error of judgment?

It also mistakes the purpose of guidance. God wants us to grow to trust him and to walk in fellowship with him. Wisdom is a practical skill which only develops as it is exercised.

What about genuine mistakes made in good faith after prayer and wise counsel? Sometimes God allows us to make decisions which, with the wisdom that hindsight brings, would probably have gone differently. But such decisions do not leave us stranded for life. They lead us on to maturity. When my children were small, my wife and

I made most of their decisions for them. As they grew older, we set options before them and encouraged them to think through the consequences. Sometimes they made mistakes. But they learned from these mistakes and grew towards wisdom and maturity.

Even when we act in a foolish way, Jesus brings his grace into our situation. Steve Tamayo writes:

> I've made foolish decisions in my life, and perhaps you have as well. I've learned from some of them and seen God's grace. My sensitivity to God's voice and his Spirit's leading has grown. I've gotten to know myself better: my strengths and temptations.[1]

To clarify our thinking, we need to ask: What do we mean by 'the will of God'?

The Bible gives at least two answers to this question.

1 God's sovereign will

The first way in which the Bible speaks about the will of God is in terms of his perfect sovereign will.

God has an eternal and all-embracing plan which cannot be defeated and which will result in his glory and the good of his people. Everything that happens in this world is the result of this plan. His sovereign plan is comprehensive, mysterious and invincible. It covers everything in creation, from quarks to galaxies and from earthworms to angels. The history of the world is not a series of meaningless random events. They are the outworking of God's plan. His purpose encompasses the cosmos, the human race, the church and every individual who has ever lived or who will ever live. All things are conformed to his will (Eph. 1:11).

It is of the very essence of God that his plans cannot fail:

> Remember the former things, those of long ago;
> I am God, and there is no other;
> I am God, and there is none like me.
> I make known the end from the beginning,
> from ancient times, what is still to come.

I say, 'My purpose will stand,
>   and I will do all that I please.'
(Isaiah 46:9–10)

Probably the greatest confession of this comes from the lips of a pagan king. In his pride, Nebuchadnezzar, the king of Babylon, had boasted of the magnificence of his own glory and majesty. In response to such a reckless and arrogant claim, God removed his sanity and brought him face to face with his human frailty. After a period of humiliation, the king returned to his senses and recognized that the Lord is king, not him!*

> At the end of that time, I, Nebuchadnezzar, raised my eyes towards heaven, and my sanity was restored. Then I praised the Most High; I honoured and glorified him who lives for ever.
>
> His dominion is an eternal dominion;
> >   his kingdom endures from generation to generation.
> All the peoples of the earth
> >   are regarded as nothing.
> He does as he pleases
> >   with the powers of heaven
> >   and the peoples of the earth.
> No one can hold back his hand
> >   or say to him: 'What have you done?'
> (Daniel 4:34–35)

This great truth is the softest pillow on which we can rest our heads. When it comes to guidance, I do not have to be fatalistic – God expects me to think and act; I am not a puppet. But neither do I need to be afraid. Even my errors can be overruled by God. His plan encompasses all my decisions, even the bad ones. Of course, I do not

---

* You can find the story in Daniel 4. It looks as if this pagan king had been converted as he bowed the knee to the God of Daniel.

want to make bad decisions, but I am fallible and occasionally I may get bad advice or fail to take in all the factors or just act in a stupid way. But this cannot derail God's plan. I know that his plan for me is always for my good.

His people are precious to him. We can trust him, even when we cannot readily discern the direction of his purposes. Even risky decisions of faith will not faze him. I am writing at the time of a coronavirus lockdown. There are several barmy theories flying round the internet at the moment about God's purposes with regard to Covid. I do not have the temerity to pretend that I can act as an infallible spokesman for God on this subject. However, I can say definitively that Covid did not take God by surprise and it did not somehow find a way under his radar. It is within his purpose to grow his church and do his people good. He will build his church and the gates of hell will not prevail against it (Matt. 16:18).

God's plans are always good. The word 'good' means 'worthy of approval'. The goodness of God means that God is the final standard of good and that everything God does is worthy of approval. His plans are also wise. God's wisdom mean that he always chooses the best goals and the best means of achieving those goals. With our limited view, we cannot always see this. Sometimes heavenly plans make no earthly sense, but we can always trust the wisdom of God. Remember the cross!†

We do not know God's sovereign will in advance, but we can trust that he is working all things for the good of those who love him (Rom. 8:28).

2 God's revealed will

But there is a second way in which the Bible describes the will of God. This is referred to as God's revealed will or his will of desire. It is what he has revealed in Scripture.[2] It tells us how God has commanded us to live. It tells us who God is and what he wants of his

---

† 1 Corinthians 1:18–31. The message of the cross appears foolish, but it is the ultimate demonstration of God's wisdom. We can only know this as we look back from the perspective of the resurrection. It is as we look back over our lives that we will one day see that in his wisdom God did all things well.

creatures. It is all that we need in order to know God and to live a life that is pleasing to him. Whereas God's sovereign will can never be frustrated, we can and do resist his revealed will. This is the essence of sin.

When it comes to guidance the Bible, rightly understood, gives us all we need to make good and wise decisions.

God is perfectly at liberty to direct our lives in ways that are beyond Scripture. Most of us can probably remember a few occasions when something quite extraordinary has led us to make decisions which, with hindsight, we would never have reached in any other way. An unexpected providence, an overwhelmingly strong impression or the intervention of a wise friend has changed the course of our lives. However, living our lives by these things alone, and not being firmly grounded in Scripture, will inevitably lead to frustration.

What God does promise and what he regularly does is to guide us through Scripture. As we will see in a later chapter, there are right and wrong ways of using the Bible. All I want to affirm here is that all we ever need to know of God's plan for our lives is revealed in the Scriptures. Many of our decisions will be straightforward because the Bible gives a clear direction or a prohibition. All we have to do is obey. Most of our decisions are morally neutral – we could easily choose between several options and still please God. They are 'wisdom calls', and the Bible promises to help us to decide wisely.

Is there more?

That leads us back to where we started. Is there a third use of the term 'will of God' in the Bible? Does the Bible reveal that God has a specific will for each of our lives which can be discovered and then followed or resisted? Has God devised an ideal plan, designed perfectly for me, which takes me from cradle to grave? If he has, how do I discover it, and what if I get it wrong? Taking a false turn in my sixties might have dire consequences, but that is nothing compared with missing God's best in my twenties. I am then doomed to a life of mediocrity. God still loves me – but I am never going to realize all the possibilities he may have designed for me. I can only ever experience God's second best.

We might call this the 'secret plan' view. Gerald Sittser describes it like this:

> Conventional understanding of God's will defines it as a specific pathway we should follow into the future. God knows what this pathway is, and he has laid it out for us to follow. Our responsibility is to discover this pathway – God's plan for our lives . . . If and when we make the right choice, we will receive his favour, fulfil our divine destiny and succeed in life . . . If we choose wrongly, we may lose our way, miss God's will for our lives, and remain lost forever in an incomprehensible maze.[3]

This view of guidance demands something beyond the Bible.

In the traditional view, God speaks directly to us through the Scriptures as they are interpreted by our renewed minds under the direction of the Holy Spirit. It is then up to us to come to a decision and act upon it. There is a direct line to us from God via the Bible though our surrendered minds.

The 'secret plan' view adds another link in the chain. Between the Bible and me there are certain signs or markers which make God's general will in the Bible particular and specific to me and my circumstances. Such signs may involve subjective impressions, prearranged signs, extra-biblical words from God, open doors or something else. I don't want to deny that any of these things are possible. I would simply plead that they should be tested by Scripture. The Holy Spirit is sovereign and can guide us as he chooses. He is also consistent and will never contradict his words in the Bible.

Some of the so-called signs are decidedly dodgy – what do we mean by a fleece and how do we test a subjective conviction? But it seems to me that the greatest danger is that they undermine our confidence in God's goodness and the reliability of his revelation in Scripture. An unhealthy preoccupation with the future and a desire for a certainty which God does not promise can prevent us from walking by faith. In the end, it is a matter of trust.

God has a plan, but he does not burden us with the task of understanding it in every detail. God does care about my future and he does guide me and oversee the consequences of all my decisions, but he has not promised to share the itinerary with me ahead of time. A glimpse of the next few steps is all we need – we do not need to see the far horizons. We know that the end of the journey is heaven – that should inspire us when the going gets tough.

Would you really want to know the plan even if you could? Imagine God told you beforehand of the serious illness that your wife would experience in her thirties or the severity of the disability of your seventh grandson. Imagine he told you the date of your death. Would you really want this information?[‡] We could not change anything and we would probably find it too hard to handle. It is in grace that God shields us from such knowledge. Sufficient to the day are the troubles of each day (see Matt. 6:34).

If life is a journey, God wants us to learn to walk with him and enjoy the scenery. As we trust God and make decisions based on obedience to his Word, we continue to become more like Jesus. Making decisions tests the quality of our discipleship because they demand obedience to God no matter the consequences. When people say they are having problems of guidance, they often mean that they are having problems of obedience!

Jim Packer writes:

> For the truth is that God in his wisdom, to make and keep us humble, and to teach us to walk by faith, has hidden from us almost everything we should like to know about the providential purposes which he is working out in the churches and in our own lives . . .
>
> We can be sure that the God who made this marvellously complex world-order, and who compassed the great redemption from Egypt, and who later compassed the even greater redemption from sin and Satan, knows what he is doing and 'doeth all things well', even if for the moment he hides his

---

‡ In Isaiah 38 God revealed the date of his death to king Hezekiah. Read Isaiah 39 and you will see that the consequences were disastrous.

hand. We can trust him and rejoice in him, even when we cannot discern his path.[4]

We can trust God. Remember the words of Jesus: 'Therefore I tell you, do not worry about your life, what you will eat; or about your body, what you will wear' (Luke 12:22).

When we refuse to trust God, we are telling him that we do not think he is big enough or wise enough to guide us into the future. We are doubting that he can be trusted to lead us, provide for us, protect us and bring us safely home. Guidance is not supposed to be like finding our way through a labyrinth. God wants us to stop obsessing about our future and to trust him.

I was called to be the pastor of a church in Wiltshire at the age of twenty-six and I stayed there for almost fourteen years. What if I got it wrong? Like most ministries, there were good times and bad times. I confess that on at least one occasion when things were particularly tough, I wondered whether I had made a mistake. We had very few young people, and in a six-month period I conducted the funerals of ten of the church members. Was I the right man? Had I misunderstood God's will? Had I taken the wrong turn? Was I stranded in Boston?

And that is the problem with the 'secret plan' view of guidance. It produces uncertainty and doubt. I may have been right to doubt my own wisdom, but this meant doubting God. It paints the picture of an impotent God who sees me making a huge mistake and is powerless to either prevent it or turn it to good. It also assumes that once we find God's plan it will lead to a life of comparative comfort and delightful ease. There is no such guarantee for cross-bearers. What I learned in those difficult circumstances was to know and trust God better.

The dominance of this view leads to what Mark Dever calls 'spiritual and emotional bondage'. Insisting on some deep inner conviction – a sense of subjective compulsion – can lead to paralysis. I do not want to deny that sometimes God does give us a strong conviction which is counter-intuitive and yet undeniable. We will explore that later. However, I agree with Dever when he writes:

Most of the decisions I've made in my Christian life, I've made with no such sense of subjective leading. Maybe some would say that this was a mark of my spiritual immaturity. I understand this to be the way a redeemed child of God normally lives in this fallen world before the fullness of the kingdom comes, Christ returns, and immediate, constant, unbroken fellowship with God is established . . . The desire for such a subjective sense of leading, however, is too often, in contemporary evangelical piety, binding our brothers and sisters in Christ, paralyzing them from enjoying the good choices that God may provide and causing them to wait wrongly before acting.

Let's be clear. God does have a plan for our lives, but he has not revealed it to us in its entirety. Occasionally he may change our direction using extraordinary means, but most of the time he expects us to walk with him by faith and leave the working-out of our decisions in his hands. This is wonderfully liberating. I do not need to second-guess God. I can concentrate on getting to know him and understanding his clearly revealed will rather than trying to gaze into a crystal ball which shows me the blueprint of the future.

Is it possible that I might make a decision which, on reflection, looks as if it was wrong? Yes, of course this may happen in a fallen world. Does it mean I am doomed to second best? No! Here is an opportunity to grow. I learn more about God, my faith is deepened and, hopefully, I become a wiser person.

And I will never be stranded in Boston.

Questions

1 How is the view of God's sovereignty described in this chapter both a comfort and a challenge? How do I avoid fatalism?
2 Read Psalm 19. What does it imply about the nature of God's Word? What does it tell us about the benefits of God's Word?
3 How does the desire to know God's secret will lead to 'spiritual bondage'?
4 What should I do if I were to conclude that, with hindsight, a decision I had made in good faith was the wrong decision?

Part 1

UNDERSTANDING THE PRINCIPLES

Trust and obey

In the words that we quoted at the beginning of this book, Solomon describes the interplay between divine sovereignty and human responsibility when it comes to guidance:

> Trust in the LORD with all your heart
>   and lean not on your own understanding;
>   in all your ways submit to him,
>   and he will make your paths straight.
> (Prov. 3:5–6)

These are probably the most often quoted verses on the theme of guidance. They are a wonderful antidote to the paralysis that sometimes overtakes us because we are afraid of making a bad decision and ending up having to settle for God's 'second best'. God gives us three clear directions and then drives them home with a promise of guidance. Unlike some of the promises in Proverbs, the promise here is unconditional.

Think about the three conditions for a moment. If our understanding of guidance demands that we somehow discover God's secret will in every situation, we are left with something of a conundrum. What are the steps we should take? Can we ever be certain? What if we get it wrong? What Solomon does here is to give us three things that we can do. They may be difficult, but with God's grace we can obey these three commands.

What are the three directives?

1 Trust in the Lord with all your heart

The word 'trust' means to lean on, rely on or rest in. We do not know the future and we are not able to predict the consequences of every decision we make. But we do not have to! The key thing about faith is not the quality or power of the faith, but its direction. When we make our decisions, we can trust the one who has never ceased to be a reliable guide throughout our life. Past grace is a clear token of future grace. More than that, we are trusting a God who is incapable of being unfaithful. This is no excuse for foolishness, but it does embolden our decision-making. We can do this.

2 Lean not on your own understanding

One of the principal themes in Proverbs is the call to listen to the right voices. We are surrounded by a cacophony of opinions and outlooks. Our minds are soaked with and shaped by our surrounding culture. The 'wisdom' of the world is seductive. Worldly wisdom may lead to temporary success. Do not be fooled. Set your mind on God's perspective – delight in him, commit your way to him, trust him, be still before him and do not fret. The story of the fall of Adam and Eve gives a salutatory warning about listening to the wrong voices.

3 In all your ways submit to him

Third, we are to deliberately surrender our lives to the clear directions of God's revealed will. There is no point in fretting over the things we cannot know. God calls us to submit to the things we do know. God's commands are comprehensive. They may not give specific directions in every area of our lives, but they do get down to the nitty gritty of our everyday decisions. Wisdom cries out to us at street level. Work hard and obey what God makes clear and stop worrying about the outcome. Knowing God's will is clearly a challenge – but it is not our biggest challenge. The biggest challenge in the Christian life is to do God's will and to be holy.

In summary, we are called to trust and obey, and God promises to do the rest.

The promise is just as clear as the commands. He will make your paths straight. This is not the promise of an easy journey but of a safe arrival. Obedience is no guarantee of ease and comfort. However, trusting his promise, taking care to live according to his commands, seeking his will in prayer and stepping out in faith is surrounded by this promise of a straight and clear path. There is a clear demarcation of responsibilities here. I am to do what by God's grace I am called to do. God will do the rest. I do not need to become anxious about guidance, because that is his responsibility, not mine.

Solomon drives this home in Proverbs 3:7:

> Do not be wise in your own eyes;
>   fear the LORD and shun evil.

Trusting God for the future involves a humble and teachable spirit – I am not wise in my own eyes. It also involves a reverent and godly fear which leads to an aversion to evil.

In chapters 2 to 5 we will explore four principles which should help us to understand the nature of guidance. In chapter 6 we will examine some of the other factors to which people often refer – things like the open door or the fleece. Finally, in chapter 7 we will outline seven steps we might follow as we plot our way towards the goal of making decisions that please God and bring glory to him.

In the next four chapters we will work with the following definition:

God guides us through the Scriptures as they are illuminated by the Spirit in answer to persistent prayer, so that, thinking clearly, we can make wise, God-glorifying decisions.

We can break this down into four principles:

'God guides us through the Scriptures ...'

Principle 1

God guides us through the Scriptures

'... as they are illuminated by the Spirit ...'

Principle 2

God sends the Spirit to guide us

'... in answer to persistent prayer ...'

Principle 3

God guides us in answer to persistent prayer

'... so that, thinking clearly, we can make wise,
God-glorifying decisions.'

Principle 4

God promises to give us wisdom

Principle 1

GOD GUIDES US THROUGH THE SCRIPTURES

2

Listening to God

Danger: handle with care

My wife Edrie and I have known each other since junior school and were part of the same church youth group.

I guess I was sixteen when I fell in love with her.

I had the great privilege of attending a church where the Bible was loved, trusted and preached. That created in me a love for Scripture that has never left me. It also meant that a desire to know God's will was framed by my confidence that I would find the answer in the Bible.

The Bible is a wonderful gift, but it is a dangerous book when it is misused.

Daydreaming about Edrie one day, I prayed for guidance about whether I should ask her out. I opened my Bible at random and read some words in Malachi 2:14: 'You ask, "Why does he not?" Because the Lord was witness to the covenant between you and the wife of your youth, to whom you have been faithless, though she is your companion and your wife by covenant' (RSV).

The phrase 'wife of your youth' was what jumped off the page. I did not understand all the stuff about covenants and being faithless – indeed, I totally ignored the context. I took a warning as a promise. But hadn't God spoken to me? It seemed rather spooky, but I had prayed!

There must have been doubts in my mind, and I didn't share this with Edrie until after we were married!

God can use the Bible any way he wants, but I must confess that I am rather embarrassed as I look back now. The practice of seeking spiritual insight by selecting a random passage is sometimes referred to as 'bibliomancy'. A variation on the theme is the 'promise box', which was popular when I was young. It contained small, rolled-up parchments, each of which was inscribed with a wonderful promise from the Bible. Many of these promises contained gloriously comforting truths which were applicable in an almost limitless variety of situations.

All of us have found a promise that has brought amazing comfort in dark days and difficult situations. The problem comes when we make them specific to our particular situation. The promise then becomes a kind of Christian fortune cookie.

Rightly understood, any passage in the Bible can encourage and strengthen us. We have all had the experience of discovering a promise that seems to be just what we need in a given situation. But it is not a wise method of seeking guidance. At best, it is a lazy approach which substitutes the study of the Scriptures with a quick fix. At worst, it is little better than consulting a horoscope or a crystal ball.

God expects us to exercise our minds and not suspend them. I go to my doctor and tell her my symptoms. Imagine that she were to pull down a medical textbook, open it at random and tell me that I am suffering from postnatal depression. I would change my doctor!

I want a doctor who intelligently engages with my symptoms and uses her medical knowledge to come to a diagnosis. When it comes to guidance, God expects me to use my reason to engage with the Bible and to apply its principles to the choices I face.

Now, in his sovereignty, God may use even such a random method, but there is no guarantee. Remember that the main contention of this book is that God uses the process of seeking and finding guidance to deepen our relationship with him and to transform our character. This method of approach achieves neither of these ends. God gave us a brain and he expects us to use it.

There seem to be two fundamental questions to address here. First, why should we look to the Bible for guidance? Second, how should we use the Bible without misusing it?

What the Bible says, God says

God is there and he is not silent. God's will is revealed in human language. Just as my voice is carried by my breath, so the mind of God comes to us through his breath in real words which accurately communicate his will (2 Tim. 3:16–17). What the Bible says is what God says. It tells us what he wants us to believe and what he wants us to do. The Bible must overrule every other supposed means of direction.

We can have confidence that all that God wants us to know is found in the pages of the Bible. Peter tells us:

> His divine power has given us everything we need for a godly life through our knowledge of him who called us by his own glory and goodness. Through these he has given us his very great and precious promises, so that through them you may participate in the divine nature, having escaped the corruption in the world caused by evil desires.
> (2 Peter 1:3–4)

Living a life that pleases God – a godly life – comes through knowing him. The Bible gives us everything we need to live such a life. This knowledge comes to us through his 'very great and precious promises'. And, of course, these promises come to us through the Bible. The Bible teaches, rebukes, corrects and trains us in righteousness so that we can be 'thoroughly equipped for every good work' (2 Tim. 3:17).

What we have in the Bible is the full and final revelation of God's will for our lives. We do not need anything else. We must not add or subtract from the words God has given us. He does not tell us everything that we might want to know, but he tells us everything we need to know. 'The secret things belong to the LORD our God, but the things revealed belong to us and to our children for ever, that we may follow all the words of this law' (Deut. 29:29).

The Bible is the supreme vehicle of guidance. We often crave the certainty of vivid impressions or dramatic providences or open doors. We are not claiming that God does not continue to speak in other ways, but no contemporary 'word' from God is to be placed on a level with Scripture. He will never guide us to do anything or believe anything that contradicts the Bible.

The Bible is not just for the 'experts' – it is food for all God's people. Some parts of the Bible may be difficult to understand, but the basic thrust of its message is attainable to every child of God. We are to teach it to our children (Deut. 6:6–7) and meditate on it day and night (Ps. 1:2), knowing that it makes simple people wise (Ps. 19:7). The main things are the plain things, and the plain things are the main things.

When it is interpreted correctly, it reveals all we need to know to please God. But here's the rub. It is entirely possible to have a true understanding of the origin and nature of the Bible and to approach it with reverence and humility and yet to misuse it in such a serious way that we end up following our own will rather than God's.

John Newton counsels:

> In general, he (God) guides and directs his people by affording them, in answer to prayer, the light of his Holy Spirit, which enables them to understand and to love the Scriptures. The word of God is not used as a lottery; nor is it designed to instruct us by shreds and scraps, which, detached from their proper place, have no determinative import; but it is to furnish us with just principles, right apprehensions to regulate judgement and affections, and thereby to influence and direct our conduct.[1]

The Bible is not a portable life coach or a detailed blueprint for every minor detail of our lives or an infallible lucky dip.

So how should we use the Bible?

Hearing God

If we want to discover God's will in Scripture, we need to give God time to speak to us. In our study of the Bible, we need to respect the normal rules of interpretation.[2] 'The Bible is not an anthology of unrelated texts, but a cumulative historical revelation.'[3]

More than this, we need to meditate on God's Word:

> Keep this Book of the Law always on your lips; meditate on it day and night, so that you may be careful to do everything written in it. Then you will be prosperous and successful.
> (Joshua 1:8)

Meditation does not mean emptying our mind. It means filling our mind with Scripture and turning it over again and again as we pray and think of the implications of what we have read.

We all have specific questions that we want to ask. But the Bible seems to speak only in general terms. It does not give us the name of the woman we are to marry or the career path we are to follow. So what do we do?

Let me suggest three things.

1 The knowledge of God's grand design

The Bible helps us to make wise decisions by revealing God's purposes for the world.

One of the biggest challenges in guidance is trying to escape from the mean little cell of my own ego. Sin means that we are curved in on ourselves. We are dominated by our own felt needs and desires. When we are faced with major decisions we are driven by our own plans, comforts and selfish ambitions. We think that the world revolves around us. In the Bible, God pulls us back into shape. He reminds us of what his grand designs are for the world, for the church and for our lives. It's not all about me and what I want. Understanding God's grand design will revolutionize our decision-making. It will challenge the questions we usually ask and provide us with a series of new ones.

Instead of asking:

- How does this affect me?
- How does this contribute to my self-esteem?
- How can I avoid pain and find comfort?

We begin to ask:

- How does this fit in with God's plan for his world?
- What will please him most?
- What will bring him glory?

But what is God's grand design? What is the big picture?

God is building a family of men and women who are being transformed to be like Jesus. 'For those God foreknew he also predestined to be conformed to the image of his Son, that he might be the firstborn among many brothers and sisters' (Rom. 8:29).

This was the purpose of the incarnation. Jesus Christ took flesh and blood and experienced temptation, pain and death in order to fulfil God's purpose of restoring the human race to the glory they had experienced before Adam's fall:

> In bringing many sons and daughters to glory, it was fitting that God, for whom and through whom everything exists, should make the pioneer of their salvation perfect through what he suffered. Both the one who makes people holy and those who are made holy are of the same family. So Jesus is not ashamed to call them brothers and sisters.
> (Heb. 2:10–11)

God is building his church and extending his kingdom. Jesus promised, 'And I tell you that you are Peter, and on this rock I will build my church, and the gates of Hades will not overcome it' (Matt. 16:18).

History is the scaffolding behind which God is forming the family of his church. We are part of that building project.

Beyond this, God has declared that he will bring about a new creation – a world purged of sin and perfected in glory. It is the hope of sharing in this kingdom that lightens every load and should govern every decision. The more we understand God's grand design, the less self-centred our decisions will be and the more they will glorify God. Where I work, how I spend my time and my money, what church I attend, will all come under the compass of God's grand design.

So whether you eat or drink or whatever you do, do it all for the glory of God. Do not cause anyone to stumble, whether Jews, Greeks or the church of God – even as I try to please everyone in every way. For I am not seeking my own good but the good of many, so that they may be saved.
(1 Cor. 10:31–33)

2 God's directions

Once we have grasped something of God's character and his purpose, we can move on to the specific directions that he gives in the Bible. The Bible tells us everything we need to know and everything we need to do to please God. In many cases the directions are crystal clear and unambiguous.

We may distinguish two types of direction:

(a) Prohibitions

Prohibitions are negative commands telling us what we should not do.

Most of the Ten Commandments take this form and forbid things such as idolatry, blasphemy, murder, adultery, theft, stealing and covetousness. In the New Testament we find more-specific prohibitions:

Therefore each of you must put off falsehood and speak truthfully to your neighbour, for we are all members of one body. 'In your anger do not sin': do not let the sun go down while you are still angry, and do not give the devil a foothold. Anyone who has been stealing must steal no longer, but must work, doing something useful with their own hands, that they may have something to share with those in need.
(Eph. 4:25–28)

Notice here that Paul gives a positive alternative to a forbidden action.

In making decisions, I must refrain from breaching these prohibitions at all times and in all situations. The Bible contains unchanging moral absolutes. God has revealed these principles and we must obey.

So, for example, I cannot decide to desert and divorce my wife and start living with another woman, because the seventh Commandment forbids this. I cannot take a job, no matter how lucrative, if I discover that I will regularly be expected to lie or act in a dishonest way.

This is pretty straightforward. No new word from God or unexpected providence or apparently miraculous intervention should cause me to make any decision that breaches a clear biblical prohibition. Christians sometimes get themselves tied up in knots *feeling* God's leading in one direction but *seeing* an explicit command in another. God never contradicts himself. If your feelings contradict God's Word, you can be sure that your feelings are mistaken.

(b) Commands

The Bible contains many positive commands which should direct our lives and shape our decisions.

Think of the commands of Jesus:

> But seek first his kingdom and his righteousness, and all these things will be given to you as well.
> (Matt. 6:33)

> A new command I give you: love one another. As I have loved you, so you must love one another.
> (John 13:34)

> Go and make disciples of all nations, baptising them in the name of the Father and of the Son and of the Holy Spirit, and teaching them to obey everything I have commanded you.
> (Matt. 28:19–20)

Or take the following commands of Paul:

> Rejoice always, pray continually, give thanks in all circumstances; for this is God's will for you in Christ Jesus.
> (1 Thess. 5:16–18)

Live a life worthy of the Lord and please him in every way:
bearing fruit in every good work.
(Col. 1 :10)

Be filled with the Spirit, speaking to one another with psalms,
hymns, and songs from the Spirit.
(Eph. 5:18–19)

Gerald Sittser comments:

And what is that will of God? Is it some specific, secret plan
God has for us and wants us to spend days weeks even years
discovering? Not at all. Rather it consists of a sober life, living
in the power of the Holy Spirit, and offering praise and gratitude to God for his goodness. Paul's main concern is about
how believers conduct themselves in ordinary life.[4]

Let's focus on one specific command. In 1 Thessalonians 4:3 Paul
writes, 'It is God's will that you should be sanctified: that you should
avoid sexual immorality.'

The prohibition in the second half of the verse is quite specific and
forbids any form of sexual activity outside the confines of a lifelong marriage relationship between one man and one woman. The
command in the first part of the verse is much more general and all
embracing. In every decision I make I know that God's will is that I
should be holy, as he is holy (Lev. 11:44–45; 1 Pet. 1:15–16). This
process may be painful as the master potter shapes our lives, but the
pressures of life are the hands of the potter. Agonizing over decisions
and learning from our mistakes is part of the higher goal of trans-
forming our characters.

What does this mean in practice? By the power of God's Spirit
we are being transformed into the likeness of Jesus Christ. In
Christ we see God as he truly is and human beings as they were
meant to be. The Bible calls us to be like Christ in all our decisions
and desires. Transformation into his likeness is God's ultimate goal
for our lives.

Consider the following five directions:

Love. Ephesians 5:1–2: 'Follow God's example, therefore, as dearly loved children and live a life of love, just as Christ loved us and gave himself up for us as a fragrant offering and sacrifice to God.'

Forgiveness. Colossians 3:13: 'Bear with each other and forgive one another if any of you has a grievance against someone. Forgive as the Lord forgave you.'

Endurance. Hebrews 12:2–3: '. . . fixing our eyes on Jesus, the pioneer and perfecter of faith. For the joy that was set before him he endured the cross, scorning its shame, and sat down at the right hand of the throne of God. Consider him who endured such opposition from sinners, so that you will not grow weary and lose heart.'

Generosity. 2 Corinthians 8:7, 9: 'But since you excel in everything – in faith, in speech, in knowledge, in complete earnestness and in the love we have kindled in you – see that you also excel in this grace of giving . . . For you know the grace of our Lord Jesus Christ, that though he was rich, yet for your sake he became poor, so that you through his poverty might become rich.'

Humility. Philippians 2:5–7a: 'In your relationships with one another, have the same mindset as Christ Jesus:

> who, being in very nature God,
> > did not consider equality with God something to be used
> > > to his own advantage;
> rather, he made himself nothing . . .'

If Christ has won our hearts, then we will want to make decisions that are shaped by a desire to be like him. Should I take this job? Which church should I join? How should I use my money? As I muse over every decision, I am constrained by a desire to think and act like Jesus. My decisions are to be marked by the attributes described above.

As we consider these commands, we need to establish priorities. We may obey some of them at all times – like the command to be holy or to seek God's kingdom. But what about when the command is more specific? Consider an example. The Bible commands me as a Christian to join together with God's people (Heb. 10:24–25). It also commands me as a father not to exasperate my children (Eph. 6:4). When I arrive home in the evening I plan to go to the home group so that I can obey the command about fellowship. But my son has had a really tough day and he needs some time with his dad. Going to another meeting might exasperate him. I have to decide on the basis of priorities in this situation. This requires wisdom and discernment. The Bible promises to help us to develop these qualities, as we shall see in chapter 5.

3 Matters of liberty

What if there is neither a command nor a prohibition?

Many decisions are matters of liberty. They are morally neutral. In these situations, we are free to choose between one or more equally good alternatives.

For example, taking a teaching job in Birmingham or Bradford is a wisdom call. Provided that I am not violating any commands or ignoring any prohibitions, I am free to choose. Now one choice might be wiser than another and I have to make an informed decision based on all the data I can gather, but neither choice is commanded or forbidden in the Bible and God expects me to use my common sense and then go for it.

Paul helps us here. He directs us to ask two questions about morally neutral decisions.

(a) Is it beneficial?

'I have the right to do anything,' you say – but not everything is beneficial.
(1 Cor. 6:12)

Certain actions may not be wrong in themselves, but they do not encourage Christian growth and maturity. Taking a high-powered job, for example, may not be forbidden, and may be a place where I might exercise a healthy Christian influence. But what if it is so demanding that I begin to neglect my personal relationship with God and start to drift away from him? I need to know myself. You might flourish under pressure and have strong self-discipline which means that you will never neglect prayer. But I might struggle, with dire consequences for my spiritual life. It would not be beneficial for me to take the job.

This is where guidance becomes a matter of sanctified common sense that is framed by self-knowledge and a desire to please God. Different people will come to different conclusions. Should I buy a season ticket to watch West Bromwich Albion play? I might find it relaxing and I may meet lots of non-Christians. Both of those are good things. But what if it begins to control me? What if I suffer mood swings and football becomes an idol of the heart? Idols have to be pulled down. What might be fine for you may not be fine for me.

(b) Is it loving?

In 1 Corinthians 8, Paul addresses the question of eating meat offered to idols. He sees this as a morally neutral issue since an idol is nothing (1 Cor. 8:1–6). But not everyone shares this view, and he will do nothing – even in the name of liberty – that might cause another person to stumble and fall into sin:

> Be careful, however, that the exercise of your rights does not become a stumbling block to the weak. For if someone with a weak conscience sees you, with all your knowledge, eating in an idol's temple, won't that person be emboldened to eat what is sacrificed to idols? So this weak brother or sister, for whom Christ died, is destroyed by your knowledge. When you sin against them in this way and wound their weak conscience, you sin against Christ. Therefore, if what I eat causes my brother or sister to fall into sin, I will never eat meat again, so that I will not cause them to fall.
> (1 Cor. 8:9–13)

No man is an island. We do not live for ourselves alone. My actions may affect others in a negative way, causing them to stumble. Loving my neighbour overrides my liberty.

Our aim as Christians is to have our wills directed by the will of God in Scripture. The principal application to guidance in this chapter is very simple: God will never direct you against his Word. Never! The Holy Spirit is consistent with himself and he will never deviate from the book that he has inspired. In an age that is suspicious of giving clear direction and which seems to suggest that we have all the resources within ourselves to answer our own questions, the Bible is unmistakably directional. At the same time, God expects us to approach it with humility, prayer and sanctified reason. It is a million miles away from the lucky dip method we began with. In the Scriptures, God draws near to us and says, 'This is the way – walk in it' (Isa. 30:21).

God guides us through the Scriptures: checklist

1 Recognize that the Bible is reliable, comprehensive and accessible. In the Bible, God has told us everything we need to make decisions pleasing to him.

2 The Bible reveals the character of God – we should meditate on his character as we make our decisions.

3 The Bible reveals the plan of God – we should meditate on his plans as we make our decisions.

4 No decision should ever breach a clear biblical prohibition.

5 In our decisions, we must always try to be directed by the commands of Scripture, but sometimes we may have to work out an order of priorities in which we obey.

6 In matters of liberty we should ask of any given action, is it beneficial, and is it loving?

Questions

1 In what ways might we misuse the Bible? Why is this
  dangerous? How can we avoid it?
2 What is God's 'grand design' for the world? Where do we fit in?
  How should this affect our choices and decisions?
3 Look at the five characteristics of the life of Jesus outlined
  in the section entitled 'God's directions'. How would these
  characteristics shape the three decisions mentioned there?
  'Should I take this job?' 'Which church should I join?'
  'How should I use my money?'
4 Think about a decision you are facing at the moment. Is there
  anything in this chapter that should affect the outcome of
  your choice?

Principle 2

GOD SENDS THE SPIRIT TO GUIDE US

3

Led by the Spirit

When God steps in

Raymond Edman, a young missionary, staggered out of the Ecuadorian jungle. He was desperately ill, and the doctor gave him little chance of recovery. In the tropics, funerals take place immediately, so his young wife dyed her wedding dress black in preparation for the inevitable. Thousands of miles away in Boston, Edman's friend, Joseph Evans, was in a prayer meeting. Suddenly, as he prayed, he had an overwhelming burden to pray for Edman. The impression was so irresistible that he interrupted the prayer meeting and shared his concerns.

The group prayed passionately for Edman. After some time, Evans sensed that their prayers had been answered. He cried out, 'Praise the Lord! The victory is won!'

Against all the odds Edman recovered. He went on to become the fourth President of Wheaton College in Illinois and senior vice president of the Billy Graham Evangelistic Association.[1]

I guess we have all heard stories like this. Many of us may have participated in them. Some people seem to speak of an almost daily experience of this kind of supernatural intervention.

What are we to make of this? Is it the normal way in which God guides? Is it a sign of special spirituality that brings a person into such a close relationship with the Holy Spirit that they have a hotline to heaven? Or is it merely a fantasy? Is it of God or the devil or just a human construction? Is it the result of hormonal balance, insomnia, medication or eating too much cheese at bedtime?

We need the guidance of the Spirit. There is a hymn that begins with the request

> Come, gracious Spirit, heavenly Dove,
> With light and comfort from above;
> Be Thou our Guardian, Thou our Guide,
> O'er every thought and step preside.[2]

The hymnwriter acknowledges that part of the Spirit's work is to be our guardian and guide. He guards us from the consequences of our foolish decisions and guides our steps in God's way. God is the Shepherd who covenants to guide his sheep and promises to seek them and bring them back when they stray onto dangerous paths. The voice of the Shepherd is the voice of the Spirit. The sheep recognize the Shepherd's voice:

> The one who enters by the gate is the shepherd of the sheep. The gatekeeper opens the gate for him, and the sheep listen to his voice. He calls his own sheep by name and leads them out. When he has brought out all his own, he goes on ahead of them, and his sheep follow him because they know his voice. (John 10:2–4)

The question before us in this chapter is, how we are to recognize the voice of the Shepherd. Is it to be identified with 'inner promptings', like the ones described above, or is it found elsewhere? Does the Spirit give supernatural words of knowledge to us or to someone else to pass on to us? Are there church leaders who are closer to the Spirit than we are and to whom we should look for spiritual direction?

In this chapter, we will explore the ways in which the Holy Spirit guides us.

Knowing the Spirit

We need to begin with a clear understanding about the identity of the Spirit.

The Holy Spirit is the third Person of the Holy Trinity. The Bible makes it clear that he is a divine Person. In his deity he is co-equal and co-eternal with the Father and the Son. He is not a force or a power but shares personal characteristics with the other members of the Trinity. He decides and plans, and he speaks and acts. As a Person, he can be blasphemed (Mark 3:29) or resisted (Acts 7:51) or quenched (1 Thess. 5:19).

Jesus promised that the Spirit would lead us into all truth. He has the particular role of directing us and empowering us to know and do the will of God. He therefore has a vital role when we think about guidance. And because he is personal, we must cultivate a relationship with him. In Ephesians, Paul writes:

> Do not let any unwholesome talk come out of your mouths, but only what is helpful for building others up according to their needs, that it may benefit those who listen. And do not grieve the Holy Spirit of God, with whom you were sealed for the day of redemption. Get rid of all bitterness, rage and anger, brawling and slander, along with every form of malice.
> (Eph. 4:29–31)

Paul warns us about our words (4:29) and our heart attitudes (4:31). He wraps these injunctions around a command not to grieve the Spirit. 'Grieve' is a love word, reminding us that the Spirit is a Person, not a force or an object. We should be sensitive to his promptings and submit to his directions contained in the Bible. He is holy, so when we are impure, we cause him grief. He is gracious, so when we are bitter or unforgiving, we sadden him. He is the Spirit of truth, so our hypocrisy and untruthfulness distress him. Whenever we pit him against Scripture, claiming that he has told us to do something that contradicts the Scriptures, we aggrieve him. We honour him when we honour the book he inspired. We also grieve him when we fail to see that the focus of his ministry is to glorify Christ (John 16:13–14).

Jim Packer expresses it like this:

It is as if the Spirit stands behind us, throwing light over our shoulder on to Jesus who stands facing us. The Spirit's message to us is never, 'Look at me; listen to me; come to me; get to know me', but always, 'Look at him, and see his glory; listen to him and hear his word; go to him and have life; get to know him and taste his gift of joy and peace.' The Spirit, we might say, is the matchmaker, the celestial marriage broker, whose role it is to bring us and Christ together and ensure that we stay together.[3]

We honour the Spirit when we glorify Christ, and as we do so, he transforms us into the likeness of Christ.

Guidance is more than making decisions – it is about knowing God. It is essentially relational, and a growing relationship with God is a prerequisite to seeking to know his will. So when it comes to seeking his help in our decision-making, we must make sure that we are cultivating a healthy relationship with the Spirit. This involves confessing all known sins and bringing our hearts into submission to his words in Scripture. As we live in submission to his prompting, he directs our paths.

But how does he direct our paths?

The Spirit and the Word

I love to preside at weddings. For me, the most solemn and joyful moment occurs when the young couple have finished making their vows and are poised before the public kiss. As the minister, I deliberately pause and look out on the congregation and declare, 'Therefore, what God has joined together, let no one separate.'

They are joined. They are about to become one flesh. They belong together. Messing with their union is messing with God's plan and purpose. Don't do it!

The same is true of the Spirit and the Word. They belong together.

We have already seen that most of our guidance comes through the Scriptures. There is an intimate relationship between the Spirit and the Word. We may break it down into four sections.

1 The Spirit wrote the Word

The God of the Bible is a God who speaks (Gen. 1:3, 6, 9, 11, 14, 20, 24, 26, 29; Ps. 33:6). He created the universe by the power of his word. The universe is the result of a sermon! Jesus Christ is his final word (Heb. 1:1–2). The Bible is God speaking in such a direct and personal way that we can be sure that we have heard his voice. It is the Word of God (Mark 7:13; Rom. 10:17; Heb. 4:12; 1 Thess. 2:13).

The Bible is the result of the outbreathing of God. It is the words and not just the ideas or the general spirit of the message that is breathed out by God. We can be confident that when we read it, we are hearing the voice of God.

Jesus promised that the Spirit would act as a counsellor who would lead his disciples into all truth: 'The Counselor, the Holy Spirit, whom the Father will send in my name, he will teach you all things, and bring to your remembrance all that I have said to you' (John 14:26 RSV). And:

> But when he, the Spirit of truth, comes, he will guide you into all the truth. He will not speak on his own; he will speak only what he hears, and he will tell you what is yet to come.
> (John 16:13)

This is not a blanket promise of guidance for all Christians. It is a specific assurance to the Apostles that when they come to author the New Testament they will experience the Spirit's guidance. The Bible did not simply fall from heaven. It was not dictated in some form of automatic writing. The Holy Spirit had a special role in this process of inspiration: 'prophets, though human, spoke from God as they were carried along by the Holy Spirit' (2 Pet. 1:21).

In Acts, the word 'carried' is used to describe a wind carrying a ship (Acts 27:15, 17). The Holy Spirit so guided the human authors that their original manuscripts were without error. That is why Scripture is reliable.

What does this mean for the subject of guidance?

The Spirit will never contradict the Bible. Never. It may sound very pious to say that the Spirit has spoken directly to us. The Spirit is God, and we worship him; the Bible is not God and it is not the object of adoration. In a choice between a written word and a personally experienced contemporary word, surely, we should go with the latter. But this is a false dichotomy. We honour the Spirit when we honour the Word. We trust the Spirit when we trust the Word.

2 The Spirit illuminates the Word

The Spirit illuminates the Scriptures so that we can understand them and apply them to our lives. When it comes to guidance, he enables us to grasp the implications of the Bible for the decisions we are facing. While on earth, Jesus himself fulfilled this role: 'he explained to them what was said in all the Scriptures the things concerning himself' (Luke 24:27).

Since Pentecost, it is the Holy Spirit who fulfils this role. He has been given so that 'we may understand what God has freely given us' (1 Cor. 2:12). It therefore follows that we should pray diligently and trustingly for the Spirit's illumination. We see this in many of Paul's prayers. For example, in Ephesians 1 he prays:

> I keep asking that the God of our Lord Jesus Christ, the glorious Father, may give you the Spirit of wisdom and revelation, so that you may know him better. I pray that the eyes of your heart may be enlightened in order that you may know the hope to which he has called you, the riches of his glorious inheritance in his holy people, and his incomparably great power for us who believe.
> (Eph. 1:17–19a)

It is the Spirit of wisdom and revelation who opens the eyes of our hearts so that we can grasp our hope and inheritance and God's power.

The Spirit is like a guide in the Tower of London who leads his audience into the presence of the Crown Jewels and explains their value and worth. The difference is that, in Christ, these treasures belong to us! As he unpacks these treasures, it will affect our decisions in a significant way.

This illuminating work of the Holy Spirit depends on our relationship with God. This is why sin can hinder our understanding of Scripture. Sin disrupts our relationship with the Spirit by grieving him. Sin causes us to resist the voice of the Spirit in the Scriptures. The more we resist, the deafer we become. We must therefore allow him to shape our lives by the power of his Word.

3 The Spirit uses the Word

The Bible is the 'sword of the Spirit' (Eph. 6:17). He uses the Word to transform our lives. It is the surgeon's scalpel in his hand which performs surgery on our souls.

> For the word of God is alive and active. Sharper than any double-edged sword, it penetrates even to dividing soul and spirit, joints and marrow; it judges the thoughts and attitudes of the heart. Nothing in all creation is hidden from God's sight. Everything is uncovered and laid bare before the eyes of him to whom we must give account.
> (Heb. 4:12–13)

The Word pierces our souls and judges our motives. It is capable of cutting to the heart of things and identifying our thoughts and intentions. A good scalpel is sharp. This allows incisions to be made that will produce little, if any, scarring. In the same way, if we allow the Word to cut away the things that are not of God, we will experience some discomfort, but we will bear no lasting scars.

In Ephesians 1:17, Paul identifies the Holy Spirit as 'the Spirit of wisdom and revelation'. He opens our understanding so that we are able to know God and grasp the nature of our inheritance. In the cut and thrust of everyday life, it is quite easy to forget who God is. The Spirit helps us to know God better. This will deepen our trust and sharpen our perception of God's presence with us. God is interested in my life (Ps. 8:3–4; Matt. 10:29–31), and I should submit to his sovereign will (Jas 4:15 1 Pet. 3:17).

The Spirit also helps us to see our inheritance and the reality of our hope:

> For our light and momentary troubles are achieving for us an eternal glory that far outweighs them all. So we fix our eyes not on what is seen, but on what is unseen, since what is seen is temporary, but what is unseen is eternal.
> (2 Cor. 4:17–18)

Can you see how these considerations would deeply affect our decisions?

4 The Spirit gives conviction

In his sovereignty, the Spirit sometimes speaks to us through the Word in a way that is utterly compelling and overwhelmingly personal.

God has not guaranteed to speak in such a decisive and personal way, but sometimes he does. It may be a word of comfort and a promise that he will accompany us in the direction we have taken. It may be a rebuke that stops us in our tracks. In our fear of misusing God's Word, we must never dismiss the possibility that he can speak directly and personally to our hearts.

Let me give another personal example. At my induction service, my pastor, Les Coley, spoke from Paul's farewell message to the Ephesians elders recorded in Acts 20:17–38. In his exposition he got to verse 24: 'However, I consider my life worth nothing to me; my only aim is to finish the race and complete the task the Lord Jesus has given me – the task of testifying to the good news of God's grace.'

At that point, he leaned across the pulpit and addressed me personally: 'In the days ahead there may be many discouragements as well as encouragements. Here is the Lord's word to you. Keep going. Don't give up! Finish the race. Keep preaching the gospel.'

It was an electrifying moment and I felt convinced that I had heard God's word for my life. I have never taken it to mean that there may never be a time when age or circumstances would prevent me from preaching. It is not an unqualified promise. However, in the last forty years it has kept me going and sustained my confidence in my calling.

Ten years into ministry, my wife became desperately ill with what turned out to be multiple sclerosis. God's Spirit spoke Psalm 18:30 into my heart: 'As for God, his way is perfect.'

This is only a fraction of the verse, which goes on to say, 'The LORD's word is flawless; he shields all who take refuge in him.'

Even now, I find it hard to put into words the comfort that those few words brought to my soul. I just knew that it was God gripping me in his strong embrace and assuring me that Edrie and I could trust him for the future. The Spirit is the Comforter, and as we seek to make God-honouring decisions, we can be sure of his presence and promptings.[4]

The concern that we do not misuse God's Word, particularly in the area of guidance, can lead to a kind of rationalism in which there is no possibility of God ever speaking in such a way. I understand the danger, and it is a real one. A text wrenched out of context and forced into our life situation can have dangerous consequences. We must never try to make the Bible say something that it does not say. The meaning of the text lies in the text, not the interpreter. But we must also make sure that we leave room for a sovereign God to speak in a way that may change the direction of our lives.

This should affect the way we understand preaching. The preacher must use all his skill to correctly interpret the Bible. If he accurately opens up the meaning of the text, then his hearers can be confident that God is speaking. But preaching is more than correct interpretation. Preaching is an event in which God draws near and speaks to his people. We should encourage a level of expectation: God will speak today; I will hear his voice; I must prepare my heart.

If guidance is all about knowing God, then reading his Word personally or hearing it publicly ought to be part of the process of decision-making. When the Bible humbles our hearts and purifies our thinking and clarifies our priorities, then we are more likely to make wise decisions. We should be open to the possibility that God will direct or redirect our paths when we meet him in his Word.

Does this mean that the Spirit will sometimes bypass our minds? Is reasoned consideration inferior to ecstatic experience?

Not at all!

Sanctified reason

The spirit sharpens our thinking. God gave us a lot of guidance when he gave us a brain!

Human beings are rational creatures. Our rationality is part of what it means to be made in the image of God. We are to love God with all our heart and soul and strength and mind (Deut. 6:4–5; Mark 12:30). Our brains are shaped and driven by the desires of our hearts, so we are not as rational and dispassionate as we sometimes think. Nonetheless, grace renews our minds (Rom. 12:1–2), and Peter commands to exercise our minds: 'Therefore, with minds that are alert and fully sober, set your hope on the grace to be brought to you when Jesus Christ is revealed at his coming' (1 Pet. 1:13).

The phrase 'with minds that are alert' is a translation of the Greek, 'gird up the loins of your mind'. It alludes to the long robes worn by men in the first century. They were impractical for vigorous work. Therefore, a belt was used to pin the robes in place around the loins, so they did not get in the way. It suggests hard and demanding thought.

Commenting on Ephesians 1:17–19, John Stott writes:

Divine illumination and human thought belong together. All our thinking is unproductive without the Spirit of truth; yet His enlightenment is not intended to save us the trouble of using our minds. It is precisely as we ponder what God has done in Christ that the Spirit will open our eyes to grasp its implications. It is commonly assumed that faith and reason are incompatible. This is not so. The two are never contrasted in Scripture, as if we had to choose between them. Faith goes beyond reason, but rests on it. Knowledge is the ladder by which faith climbs higher, the springboard from which it leaps farther.[5]

There is no excuse for an absence of vigorous and disciplined reflection. Indeed, the Spirit will sharpen our thinking so that we can grasp the meaning and application of biblical principles to our circumstances.

Does the Spirit ever bypass our reason and act in a direct and supernatural way? This certainly happened in the early church, as evidenced by the book of Acts. As we read of the first thirty years of the church's post-Pentecostal life, there are examples of visions (Acts 9:10–16; 10:10–17; 16:6–10), voices (Acts 8:26; 10:13, 15, 19–20; 23:11) and angelic appearances (Acts 8:26; 12:7–8; 27:23).

How do we assess these things?

Even in the early church, such divine interventions were not everyday occurrences. There is no indication that this was the normal means by which God guided his people. The evidence suggests that in most cases the Christians used their reason and clear biblical principles to make their plans and decisions. When faced with a massive decision concerning the admission of Gentiles (Acts 15:1–35), the church came together and, after discussion and the consideration of the biblical evidence and the prompting of circumstances, they made certain decisions. There is no evidence of visions or a special word from God. They report their decisions as resulting from the guidance of the Spirit:

> It seemed good to the Holy Spirit and to us not to burden you with anything beyond the following requirements: You are to abstain from food sacrificed to idols, from blood, from the meat of strangled animals and from sexual immorality. You will do well to avoid these things.
> (Acts 15:28–29)

There is no evidence of the early Christians asking for such guidance or of their refusal to act until God had provided some extraordinary indication of his will. They made their plans and pressed ahead and were not paralysed by the fear that they might have been making a mistake.

When God did guide in a special way, it was unmistakable. They were not left in any doubt that God had spoken. It appeared to be much more than a subjective feeling or hunch. Remember that the Holy Spirit will never prompt us to do anything that is in opposition to Scripture. Dreams, visions and hunches can seem vivid and undeniable. But if they do not conform to the Bible, they are not from God. Satan can disguise himself as an angel of light.

We should not overestimate the place of reason nor despise its importance in making wise decisions. On the one hand, we need to avoid a kind of 'deism' which says that God cannot intervene in a supernatural way. On the other hand, we must not be taken in by a form of naïve gullibility which mistrusts our sanctified reason. We must not limit God's freedom, nor must we lapse into a form of super-spiritual eccentricity. The Bible warns us to test everything: 'Do not quench the Spirit. Do not treat prophecies with contempt but test them all; hold on to what is good, reject every kind of evil' (1 Thess. 5:19–22).

Most guidance comes through the Holy Spirit enlightening our minds and enabling us to engage with the Scriptures. The Spirit, the Bible and sanctified reason are the means by which God has promised to direct our paths.

God sends the Spirit to guide us: checklist

1 We need the help of the Holy Spirit as we seek guidance.

2 Because the Spirit is a holy Person, we need to cultivate a personal relationship with him and not grieve him.

3 The Spirit wrote the Bible, and he will never contradict it.

4 The Spirit illuminates the Bible and helps us to understand it and apply it correctly.

5 Sometimes the Spirit uses the Bible in a particularly powerful way to direct our lives.

6 The Spirit can act in unexpected ways, but this is neither promised nor infallible.

7 God has given us a renewed mind and he expects us to use it.

8 The Spirit sharpens our minds and helps us to use our reason more effectively.

Questions

1 The most important truth about the Holy Spirit is that he is a divine Person. Do you think of him in personal terms? How does his personality affect the way in which we experience his ministry?

2 Why can we be sure that the Spirit will never contradict the Scriptures? Why is this principle important?

3 In what ways does the Spirit illuminate the Word? What is the role of Bible commentaries and sermons?

4 Paul talks about the Christian being 'led by Spirit' (Rom. 8:13–16; Gal. 5:18). What do you think he means by this phrase?

Principle 3

GOD GUIDES US IN ANSWER TO PERSISTENT PRAYER

4

Speaking to God

A warm invitation

As we have seen, God guides us through the Bible. But to use it properly, we need the illumination of the Holy Spirit. How do we receive the help that the Spirit gives? Contrasting earthly fathers with our heavenly Father, Jesus gives us a simple direction: 'If you then, though you are evil, know how to give good gifts to your children, how much more will your Father in heaven give the Holy Spirit to those who ask him!' (Luke 11:13).

So part of the process of guidance should involve asking God to send his Spirit to help us to understand and correctly apply the Bible. This leads us to considering the importance of prayer in seeking God's will.

In the Bible, God regularly invites his children to ask him for guidance. Think of the prayers scattered through the book of Psalms.

Lead me, LORD, in your righteousness
    because of my enemies –
    make your way straight before me.
(Ps. 5:8)

Guide me in your truth and teach me,
    for you are God my Saviour,
    and my hope is in you all day long.
(Ps. 25:5)

Since you are my rock and my fortress,
> for the sake of your name lead and guide me.
(Ps. 31:3)

Our knowledge is limited; God's knowledge is infinite. We do not know the future; God does. Our plans are flawed; God's way is perfect. We are sinful, and even in our best moments our motives are mixed; God is perfect in holiness and does all things well.

We can pray for wisdom, for direction and for purity of heart. God listens to the one who speaks and speaks to the one who listens. Someone has said that prayer is like cleaning the windscreen of your car: using your wipers enables you to see the road more clearly.[1] Prayer clears away many of the things that distort our perception and twist our motives. Prayer helps us to think more biblically and is therefore a vital factor in the process of decision-making

Learning from Jesus

Jesus gives us an example to follow. We know that decisions in his own ministry flowed from prayer:

> Very early in the morning, while it was still dark, Jesus got up, left the house and went off to a solitary place, where he prayed. Simon and his companions went to look for him, and when they found him, they exclaimed: 'Everyone is looking for you!'
>
> Jesus replied, 'Let us go somewhere else – to the nearby villages – so that I can preach there also. That is why I have come.' So he travelled throughout Galilee, preaching in their synagogues and driving out demons.
> (Mark 1:35–39)

Jesus himself spent a night in prayer before he chose the twelve Apostles (Luke 6:12–16). In Gethsemane he wrestled in prayer as he sought God's will:

Going a little farther, he fell to the ground and prayed that if possible the hour might pass from him. '*Abba*, Father,' he said, 'everything is possible for you. Take this cup from me. Yet not what I will, but what you will.'
(Mark 14:35–36)

And Jesus encouraged his disciples to pray for guidance. At the heart of the Lord's prayer is a request that our Father in heaven would guide our steps:

And lead us not into temptation,
> but deliver us from the evil one.
(Matthew 6:13)

A lot of decision-making involves more than plotting the best route and evaluating competing alternatives. Prayer grounds us. It enables us to see what is really important. Often the things that were at the top of our list of considerations appear to be less significant as we begin to think from God's perspective. Think of the opening petitions of the Lord's prayer:

Our Father in heaven,
hallowed be your name,
your kingdom come,
your will be done,
> on earth as it is in heaven.
(Matthew 6:9–10)

As I seek guidance, am I driven by a desire that God's name and reputation should be esteemed because of my decisions and choices? Is my first concern his kingdom and his righteousness (Matt. 6:33)? Do I really want God's will, or is my prayer an attempt to bend him to mine?

Praying this prayer will affect the way we make our decisions. The essential reference point will be our Father in heaven. He is our refuge and the source of our wisdom. My ultimate goal is not my pleasure or ease but his name and kingdom and glory. As I pray this prayer, I recognize my daily dependence on God.

What should we pray for?

This is the key question. When we pray for guidance, what should we ask for? To some extent, that depends on the nature of the decision facing us. There may be a different set of requests if we are seeking a church or seeking a job or seeking a spouse. We will explore this in the second part of this book.

We can pray for the wrong things. As we have seen, it is not appropriate to ask for a detailed map of the way ahead. God has not promised to reveal this. We may pray for some extra biblical confirmation of the decision we are about to make – a sign of some sort or an overwhelming sense of peace. In his grace, God may grant us these things, but once again he has not promised to do so.

There is no special formula, but our prayers may include the following:

- Tell God that you do not want to rely on your own understanding and want to submit your life to his direction (Prov. 3:5–6).
- Ask God to give you a humble heart and a teachable mind. We sometimes think that we can work out the right way to go. Even if the decision seems obvious, we should seek God's help (Ps. 25:9).
- Pray for the gift of the Spirit to illuminate the Scriptures (Luke 11:13).
- If you are anxious about the way ahead, tell God about your fears. Confess that you are afraid of making the wrong decision. Mix your petitions with thanksgiving (Phil. 4:6).
- Thank him that his grace is sufficient and that your real strength lies in knowing your own weakness and in trusting his all-sufficient grace (2 Cor. 12:9–10).
- Pray that you may be righteous so that God will direct your steps (Ps. 37:23).

- Pray that, as you consider the journey ahead of you,
  you would experience spiritual refreshment (Ps. 23:1).
- Pray that you hear his voice in the Scriptures and find the
  Bible passages that are relevant to the decision facing you
  (Ps. 119:133; John 10:27).
- Claim his promise to lead you the way ahead and thank him
  in anticipation (Isa. 48:17).
- Thank him that he has promised to guide you for the whole
  of your life (Ps. 48:14; Isa. 58:11).
- Pray that you will be contented with the direction in which
  he might guide you (John 10:27).

Praying with Paul

In his recorded prayers, Paul often asked for guidance for himself
and his readers.

> And this is my prayer: that your love may abound more and
> more in knowledge and depth of insight, so that you may be
> able to discern what is best and may be pure and blameless for
> the day of Christ, filled with the fruit of righteousness that
> comes through Jesus Christ – to the glory and praise of God.
> (Phil. 1:9–11)

Perhaps the best example of this kind of prayer is found in Colossians 1:9–12:

> For this reason, since the day we heard about you, we have
> not stopped praying for you. We continually ask God to fill
> you with the knowledge of his will through all the wisdom
> and understanding that the Spirit gives, so that you may live
> a life worthy of the Lord and please him in every way: bearing
> fruit in every good work, growing in the knowledge of God,
> being strengthened with all power according to his glorious
> might so that you may have great endurance and patience,
> and giving joyful thanks to the Father, who has qualified you

to share in the inheritance of his holy people in the kingdom of light.

This prayer falls into a primary request and a principal outcome.

1 Primary request: knowing God's will

Paul's primary request is that they might know God's will:

> For this reason, since the day we heard about you, we have not stopped praying for you. We continually ask God to fill you with the knowledge of his will through all the wisdom and understanding that the Spirit gives.
> (Col. 1:9)

Paul prays for knowledge, wisdom and understanding:

- The word 'knowledge' indicates a clear, deep, rich and full grasp of truth. It is not a superficial awareness of shallow things, but an insight into reality – things as they really are.
- It comes through 'wisdom'. Wisdom is more than an acquaintance with facts. It is knowledge rightly applied. It flows from the true knowledge of God and the fear of the Lord which this inspires.
- It is also related to 'understanding'. This word carries the idea of insight into the way in which things fit together. It is grasping the big picture. We step back from the tiny portion of the canvas to which our nose is pressed, and we see God's eternal and universal plan as it is being worked out for the cosmos, for the church and for us as individuals. It is that kind of eureka moment when we feel that we understand our place in the world and the world's place in God's grand design.

Paul is not praying for particular guidance on a specific issue. What he is praying for is a grasp of God's grand design and purpose (we dealt with this in chapter 2). What is God's heartbeat? How is his will unfolding in the events of history and of my life? God is not a pathetic observer wringing his hands in despair as he looks on a cosmos that is out of control. He is the sovereign creator and the king of the ages.

The focus of this plan is Christ. He is the source, sustainer and heir of creation. It exists for his glory. He is also the Lord of the new creation. The cosmos has been scarred by the ugly graffiti of sin, but God has not abandoned it. In Christ, God has stepped into the world he made and has begun to turn it round.

Where do I fit into this? I have been united to Christ by faith and am therefore passionately committed to all that God is doing in his world. The more I know and understand, the more I will seek to conform my life to his will, and this will involve a passion for holiness.

Although this may not have immediate relevance to the decision in hand, seeing God's plan will transform all our decisions and cut through some of the confusion we might have about guidance.

2 Principal outcome: pleasing God's heart

After this, Paul works through some of the results that flow from this knowledge:

> . . . so that you may live a life worthy of the Lord and please him in every way: bearing fruit in every good work, growing in the knowledge of God, being strengthened with all power according to his glorious might so that you may have great endurance and patience, and giving joyful thanks to the Father, who has qualified you to share in the inheritance of his holy people in the kingdom of light.
> (Col. 1:10–12)

Our overwhelming goal should be a desire to live a life that is worthy of and pleasing to God. Surely this is the heart of the question of guidance. I want to make wise decisions about my church, my job and my relationships. I want to know when to retire or start a family or enrol on a Bible training course. But overshadowing every single decision are the questions of what is worthy of God and what would really please him. Pleasing him is a matter of joyful gratitude. It is the single-minded and wholehearted desire to bring him pleasure.

We turn from the world and its desires; we turn from ourselves and our desires; we lay everything before God. We don't hold anything back: job, spouse, kids, money, our desire for security, power, influence, sexual pleasure, hobbies, sports, entertainment, friends.

But what does it look like? Paul answers this with a series of four participles.

Fruitfulness: 'bearing fruit in every good work'.

We please our Father by living fruit-bearing lives. It is to the Father's glory that we bear much fruit (John 15:8). Real fruit is always visible. It is seen in specific actions that are motivated by heart attitudes: 'But the fruit of the Spirit is love, joy, peace, forbearance, kindness, goodness, faithfulness, gentleness and self-control. Against such things there is no law' (Gal. 5:22–23).

So when I am seeking guidance, I should ask a series of questions:

- Is this decision prompted by love and kindness?
- Will this decision produce real and lasting joy and peace?
- Am I acting in a gentle way?
- Is it characterized by goodness and faithfulness?
- Am I rushing because I lack forbearance or self-control?

These may not be the kinds of questions we usually ask, but they are the ones that Paul's prayer prompts us to think through. Am I more concerned with my own comfort than with living a fruitful life? Do my decisions lead to works of mercy, grace and compassion?

Knowledge: 'growing in the knowledge of God'. Paul has already prayed that they may grow in the knowledge of God's will. One of the results of this is that once they know God's will and do God's will, they will grow in the knowledge of God himself. The knowledge of God is more than a rigorous intellectual pursuit. It flows from the fear of the Lord and a humble heart. It is attained by prayer and worship and submission to the mysteries of his providence. This knowledge is worth finding and it should control all our desires and decisions.

One of our greatest challenges is to allow our vision of God to bathe every decision we make. We need to make our decisions with a consciousness that we live our lives under the eye of this God. We need a vision of a God who is not distant or ordinary or common, but who is magnificent and breathtaking and awe-inspiring.

Character: 'being strengthened with all power according to his glorious might so that you may have great endurance and patience'.

The knowledge of God will result in a transformation of character. It is seen in endurance and patience.

Endurance involves staying put and standing firm in difficult circumstances. Life is not easy, and God calls us to endure and bring him glory even when we find ourselves under the cosh of circumstances. Sometimes the greatest glory is seen when we just keep going and do not give up. God does not just call us to start a race; he also calls us to finish a race, no matter how hard it might be. Paul writes about this in Romans 5: 'Not only so, but we also glory in our sufferings, because we know that suffering produces perseverance; perseverance, character; and character, hope' (Rom. 5:3–4).

Patience is concerned not with difficult circumstances, but with difficult people. We are very conscious of our own weaknesses and faults. We are a work in progress. And that is true of every other Christian we ever meet. We grow in character as we learn to love awkward and demanding people. We need to develop a thick skin and a tender heart.

Once again, we can use these commands as a framework for prayer as we consider guidance. Do my decisions conform to Paul's description of the way I should treat others? This is down-to-earth holiness.

Joyful thankfulness: 'giving joyful thanks to the Father, who has qualified you to share in the inheritance of his holy people in the kingdom of light'.

The final marker of a life that is lived to please God is thankfulness inspired by hope. The massive secret at the heart of the Christian faith is that it is intended to be a life not of sombre gloom, but of exuberant joy. We are called to glorify God as we enjoy him forever. It is not a matter of gritted teeth and stoic determination, but patient endurance that is infused with joy. Joy does not depend on circumstances or temperament or passing emotion. It is a deep-seated confidence in God.

Such joy is expressed in gratitude and rooted in confident hope. Our hope is fixed not on temporary and passing things. It is concentrated on an inheritance that is secure and guaranteed (1 Peter 1:3–5).

Jonathan Edwards expresses it like this:

> It becomes us to spend this life only as a journey towards heaven . . . to which we should subordinate all other concerns of life. Why should we labour for or set our hearts on anything else, but that which is our proper end and true happiness?[2]

Here is a man who is serious about the business of heaven. There is nothing else worth setting our hearts on. And such a consideration will affect every decision we ever contemplate.

> Since, then, you have been raised with Christ, set your hearts on things above, where Christ is, seated at the right hand of God. Set your minds on things above, not on earthly things. For you died, and your life is now hidden with Christ in God. When Christ, who is your life, appears, then you also will appear with him in glory.
> (Colossians 3:1–4)

Therefore we should pray that our decisions would bear good fruit, increase our knowledge of God, transform our character and lead to joyful thanksgiving. If what we decide is likely to put any of these outcomes in doubt, we should think again.

How do we pray for guidance?

Praying for guidance should be marked by perseverance. James puts it like this:

> If any of you lacks wisdom, you should ask God, who gives generously to all without finding fault, and it will be given to you. But when you ask, you must believe and not doubt, because the one who doubts is like a wave of the sea, blown and tossed by the wind. That person should not expect to receive anything from the Lord. Such a person is double-minded and unstable in all they do.
> (James 1:5–8)

For a long time, I thought that these verses were about the quality of our faith when we come to God in prayer. Being double-minded meant having a pathetically small amount of faith so that God is disappointed in us and will not listen. I have come to the conclusion that this is a misreading of what James is saying. The Bible tells us that what is important is the direction of our faith rather than its quality and quantity. God blesses small faith as we cling to him. Like the man who came to Jesus to get his son delivered from the grip of evil, we can pray, 'I do believe, help me overcome my unbelief!' (Mark 9:24). When we doubt or waver, we can ask for more faith – but a small faith will put us in contact with a great God. Our faith is not faith in faith but faith in God!

So what does James mean? I think that when he refers to the double-minded, he means people who have not resolved in their hearts that what they want more than anything else is to know and do God's will. They want guidance but are fearful of the consequences. They do not trust God to lead them in the direction that is best for them. Their will is unsurrendered. They want to use the guidance of God to further their own goals and expectations. Guidance becomes little more than a desire for God to confirm what they have already decided to do. As mentioned earlier, when people say they are having problems with guidance, they often mean that they are having problems with obedience.

How do we avoid this? We need to humble ourselves before God, for 'he guides the humble in what is right and teaches them his way' (Ps. 25:9). We need to examine our hearts. We need to ask God to search and test our hearts. We need to yield our wills to his.

God guides us in answer to persistent prayer: checklist

1 Jesus promises that the Father will give the Spirit to those who ask. We need the Spirit to help us to correctly understand and apply the Bible to the decisions we face, so we need to ask.

2 The Bible encourages us to pray for guidance.

3 Prayer helps us to get life in perspective.

4 The Lord's Prayer and the prayers of Paul help us to understand how we should pray.

5 We should pray for knowledge, wisdom and understanding.

6 We should pray that our decisions would please God.

7 We should pray that our decisions would bear good fruit, increase our knowledge of God, transform our character and lead to joyful thanksgiving.

8 We must persist in prayer.

Questions

1 Read through the Lord's Prayer and make a list of ways in which it is a good model of praying for guidance.

2 Look at the fruit of the Spirit (Gal. 5:22–23). There is one fruit with nine aspects. Look at decisions facing you at the moment. How should the fruit of the Spirit affect your current decisions?

3 How should endurance and perseverance in prayer shape our decision-making?

4 Look at Paul's prayers recorded in Ephesians 1:15–23 and
   3:14–21. What does he pray for? How might you apply these
   petitions to the way in which you pray for guidance?

Principle 4

GOD PROMISES
TO GIVE US WISDOM

5

Finding wisdom

Thank you, Dr Graham

Dr Billy Graham was once asked about how he organized his personal Bible reading. After sharing something of his method, he confessed that two books figured highly in his daily devotions. For years, Dr Graham read five Psalms and one chapter of Proverbs each day, in addition to his daily Scripture reading.

> By reading five Psalms and one chapter of Proverbs daily, you will be able to read them through each month. The Psalms will tell you how you get along with God, and the Proverbs will tell you how to get along with your fellowman.[1]

I have not followed his practice but have tried to read through the book of Proverbs at least once a year. A chapter a day for a month works well. I have found it particularly beneficial when I have faced major decisions.

We have seen that the whole Bible reveals all that God wants us to know in order to live a life that is pleasing to him. As we apply our minds to biblical revelation, we will find clear guidelines to help us with all of the questions that trouble us and all the decisions that face us.

However, there is one book in the Bible that promises to help us to discover God's will. This is the book of Proverbs, and what it promises is wisdom.

As we saw in the first chapter, although God has a plan for our lives, he does not normally reveal it in advance. Guidance comes through God making us wise. We do not seek clues that will somehow show us the secret plan. Guidance comes through the illumination of the mind and the transformation of the heart.

James Petty defines wisdom like this:

The word can be used in different ways, but I believe that wisdom is the moral skill to understand and apply the commandments of God to situations and people. It is the ability to connect the principle to the application. It particularizes and personalizes the will, priorities, and preferences of God.[2]

Wise people know how to apply the knowledge they have acquired. It is knowledge rightly applied. We are swamped with information – but we are in desperate need of wisdom. Wisdom is designed to give us the skill to live in a godly way. Wisdom acts as a stabilizing ingredient in our lives.

Wisdom is invaluable, and Proverbs promises to help us grow in wisdom. It gives us general principles which tell us, 'The world is like this – if you want to live in a way that pleases God in his world, this is the way to do it.'

The wonderful thing about the book of Proverbs is that it is comprehensive in its concerns.

Is God really interested in everyday life?

There is no area of our lives that is untouched by God's wise direction. He is concerned with our business lives and the types of scales we use and the interaction between buyer and seller:

The LORD detests dishonest scales,
    but accurate weights find favour with him.
(Prov. 11:1)

'It's no good, it's no good!' says the buyer –
    then goes off and boasts about the purchase.
(Prov. 20:14)

He directs us in our relationships, encouraging us to avoid strife and to guard our lips:

> Hatred stirs up conflict,
>> but love covers over all wrongs.
> (Prov. 10:12)

> Starting a quarrel is like breaching a dam;
>> so drop the matter before a dispute breaks out.
> (Prov. 17:14)

> Those who guard their mouths and their tongues
>> keep themselves from calamity.
> (Prov. 21:23)

He encourages us to live contented lives in which love trumps prosperity:

> Better to be a nobody and yet have a servant
>> than pretend to be somebody and have no food.
> (Prov. 12:9)

> Better a dish of vegetables with love
>> than a fattened calf with hatred.
> (Prov. 15:17)

> A heart at peace gives life to the body,
>> but envy rots the bones.
> (Prov. 14:30)

He is concerned with the way we bring up our children and the way we treat our pets:

> Discipline your children, for in that there is hope;
>> do not be a willing party to their death.
> (Prov. 19:18)

The righteous care for the needs of their animals,
    but the kindest acts of the wicked are cruel.
(Prov. 12:10)

He knows that life can be tough:

Each heart knows its own bitterness,
    and no one else can share its joy.
(Prov. 14:10)

A cheerful heart is good medicine,
    but a crushed spirit dries up the bones.
(Prov. 17:22)

He even warns us against overindulgence and tells us how to behave when we get up in the morning:

Wine is a mocker and beer a brawler;
    whoever is led astray by them is not wise.
(Prov. 20:1)

If anyone loudly blesses their neighbour early in the morning,
    it will be taken as a curse.
    (Prov. 27:14)

And this helps us when we think about guidance. Without becoming fixated on the minutiae of everyday decisions, Proverbs encourages us to see that everything falls within the orbit of God's concern. His interest is not confined to how I pray or where I worship or witness. God is interested in my friendships and my words and my hobbies and my use of time as well as my life choices. That is why Proverbs is sometimes dismissed as secular. It is secular – but that's okay because God is concerned with the secular just as much as with what we may consider to be sacred.

Proverbs operates at the level of our everyday lives. In it, the Bible puts on its overalls and goes to work.

Who is wisdom for?

This offer of wisdom is comprehensive. It is:

for giving prudence to those who are simple,
    knowledge and discretion to the young –
let the wise listen and add to their learning,
    and let the discerning get guidance.
(Prov. 1:4–5)

Wisdom is for the 'simple' and the 'young' (1:4). It is for those who are morally naïve, unformed and inexperienced in life.

The first nine chapters address this group and are framed as the directions of a wise father and mother to a son who faces all the pressures of life (1:8). They pick up on issues that might lead to foolish and self-destructive behaviour. There are severe warnings about the dangers of peer pressure (1:8–19; 2:12–14) and abundant warnings about the destructive power of uncontrolled sexual adventuring (2:16–19; 5:1–23; 6:20–35).

If all this sounds very contemporary, that is because it is! Sex, money and power continue to be factors that control our decisions and can easily misdirect our lives.

They also write for the 'wise' and 'discerning' (1:5). If we are teachable, then our treasure store of wisdom can grow. Wisdom does not automatically come with age. Is there also an implied warning here? Growing in wisdom is like running up an escalator in the wrong direction. There is only one way to successfully reach the top: you have to keep going! Wisdom is not static. The wise person is always open to new insights and always humbly seeking after more wisdom. The moment we become complacent or begin to listen to other voices, we are in danger of becoming fools. This is exactly what happened to Solomon, the wisest man in the Old Testament:

King Solomon, however, loved many foreign women besides Pharaoh's daughter . . . As Solomon grew old, his wives turned his heart after other gods, and his heart was not fully

devoted to the LORD his God, as the heart of David his father
had been.
(1 Kgs 11:1, 5–6)

In my sixties now, I pray that I might cultivate a humble and teachable heart. There is nothing more tragic than a foolish old man or
woman.

Where does wisdom begin?

The fear of the LORD is the beginning of knowledge,
   but fools despise wisdom and instruction.

Proverbs 1:7 acts as a kind of motto text for the whole book. It is
echoed a number of times throughout the book, from here at the
start to the end (31:30). If guidance is about making wise decisions,
then this is where it starts.

We live in a culture that has little respect for such an outmoded
concept as the fear of God. If God exists, then he certainly does not
expect us to fear him. He is a kind of benevolent celestial protector
who can be ignored most of the time, only to be appealed to in
trouble or blamed for disaster. At the root of this is rejection of the
God of the Bible and a misunderstanding of the nature of fear.

The God revealed in Scripture is more gracious and benevolent
than we could ever dream. At the same time, he is more awesomely
pure and holy than we could ever imagine. It is as we come to know
God as he truly is that we begin to understand why reverent awe is
the only appropriate reaction to such a God.

Fearing God goes in hand with loving and trusting him. God is
infinite and personal. As creatures of dust, we bow in awe before the
mystery of his infinite purity. As people made in his image, we long
to know him and to love him with a passionate intensity. Our relationship with God orbits these two poles, both of which are vital to
a healthy relationship with God. Like sailors who love the sea but are
aware that it is perilous, we recognize that God is good, but he is
not safe.

The fear that this God evokes involves a reverence for his majesty, a deference for his authority and a dread of his wrath. For those who can call him 'Father', it is not to be confused with abject terror. The true and wholesome fear of the Lord protects us from sin and drives away the fear of anything else. 'Moses said to the people, "Do not be afraid. God has come to test you, so that the fear of God will be with you to keep you from sinning"' (Exod. 20:20).

> Fear of man will prove to be a snare,
>> but whoever trusts in the LORD is kept safe.
> (Prov. 29:25)

Fools live without any acknowledgment of God and make their decisions bounded by human resources alone. Wise decisions are made by those who make pleasing God the Pole Star of their journey.

Reading Proverbs

To gain this wisdom we need to seek it diligently.

> My son, if you accept my words
>> and store up my commands within you,
> turning your ear to wisdom
>> and applying your heart to understanding –
> indeed, if you call out for insight
>> and cry aloud for understanding,
> and if you look for it as for silver
>> and search for it as for hidden treasure,
> then you will understand the fear of the LORD
>> and find the knowledge of God.
> (Prov. 2:1–5)

We have to mean business with God if we really want to find wisdom.

But there is a right way and a wrong way to read the book of Proverbs? How do we read it correctly?

1 String your necklace

Proverbs falls into two distinct parts. The first part of the book consists of longer meditations or sermons in praise of wisdom (Prov. 1 – 9). Apart from an acrostic poem which celebrates the wise wife (Prov. 31), the rest of the book consists of individual pithy proverbs (Prov. 10 – 30). Occasionally you may find a run of proverbs that deal with the same subject, but this is unusual. The chapters do not contain one uniting theme. They are like a series of multi-coloured beads which appear to have been strung at random to create a beautiful necklace. There is a red bead next to a blue bead. You have to count another unspecified number of beads before you find another matching red one.

If you want a necklace made up of red beads, you will need to work along the string, removing the red beads, and then rethread them.

Consider the subject of friendship. There are numerous proverbs that address this subject.[3] They come at it from a number of angles and reflect a number of perspectives. To gain a full picture you need to collect these proverbs and gain wisdom's insights about making wise choices concerning friendship. You may do this through your own reading or you might seek help from a concordance or a website that will do the work for you.[4] You might then come up with five or six summary statements to reflect different aspects of the subject.

Remember that the proverbs may seem random, but they are in a wider context that we must not ignore. The first part of the book gives us the foundation on which to read the individual proverbs. What is said there about fearing God and diligently searching for wisdom gives us the context with which to read the individual proverbs. And, of course, there is a wider biblical context – we are to read them in the light of the whole Bible. The purpose of God is to redeem us into an eternal friendship which is exemplified by Jesus, the friend who sticks closer than a brother (Prov. 18:24).

2 Don't break your teeth

Proverbs 10 – 30 is an anthology of short, pithy sayings. They are terse, vivid and poetic in form. Intended to provoke a reaction, they are marked by wit, symbolism and paradox. They are little pictures of reality, and as we read them we suddenly have a moment of recognition – 'Yes, life is exactly like that!'

We smile and know exactly what is going on when we read:

> If anyone loudly blesses their neighbour early in the morning,
>   it will be taken as a curse.
> (Prov. 27:14)

And we wince when we are reminded that:

> Hopes placed in mortals die with them:
>   all the promise of their power comes to nothing.
> (Prov. 11:7)

Proverbs are little truth bombs designed to transform the way we think about the world. This means that we have to give them time to work.

Again, they are like boiled sweets – if we try to bite them we might break our teeth. We should take as long as we need to suck out their sweetness.

Proverbs is set in the context of the home. In particular, it often takes the form of a father's instruction to his son(s).

> Listen, my sons, to a father's instruction;
>   pay attention and gain understanding.
> I give you sound learning,
>   so do not forsake my teaching.
> (Prov. 4:1–4)

This can make it sound like a male-orientated book – especially in the sections that warn about the predatory strange woman. The words of instruction also come from the lips of a mother (1:8; 4:3; 10:1). As with all Scripture, we need to heed the context but then draw out principles and applications that transcend gender, age and experience.

3 Go with the grain

When I was at school, my woodwork teacher would begin every lesson by gathering us around his work bench and repeating the same mantra: 'Remember to look after your tools and always cut the wood with the grain.'

There is a right way and a wrong way to cut wood. Cutting along the grain will make for a smoother cut and will avoid damaging the fibres.

There is a right way to cut wood, and there is a right way to 'do life'. God is the Creator as well as the Redeemer. He has made the world in a particular way. The book of Proverbs is a divinely inspired series of concise and memorable statements of general truth which cut with the grain of the way God has designed the world. They reveal the way the world is and how we are to fit into it. Since God made the world, he knows how it works, and it would be foolhardy to ignore this.

God created the law of gravity – I flout it at my peril. The physical laws of the universe are a God-given gift which make life possible. When scientists explore and articulate them, they are merely thinking God's thoughts after him. There are similar laws that govern the realm of human behaviour. Such basic principles are universal and apply to all of us. As a Christian, I am just as subject to the law of gravity as my non-Christian neighbour. The same is true in the moral realm. In most circumstances I cannot defy God's clear-cut principles of behaviour and plead exemption because of my faith.

Take as an example Proverbs 10:4: 'Lazy hands make for poverty, but diligent hands bring wealth.' This is one of a plethora of proverbs on the subject of laziness and labour. The person who refuses to work will end up in poverty; the person who works hard will, usually, acquire wealth. That's just the way the world works. It's the way God has made it. It is obvious when you think of it.

Listen to Proverbs 24:27: 'Put your outdoor work in order and get your fields ready; after that, build your house.' It is wise to make plans and decide on an order of priorities. Lunging forward in apparent planless faith is not a wise course of action. There are no excuses for ignoring the Creator's design specifications. If you try to cut against the grain you will end up with damaged wood. When it comes to guidance, don't think that you can ignore God's guidelines and still make a wise decision.

4 Cut across the grain

The proverbs describe the way that the Creator has designed his world – it is the way the world works. But not always. The world is profoundly broken and morally corrupted. That means that sometimes the expected results do not materialize.

It may be generally true that:

The fear of the LORD adds length to life,
    but the years of the wicked are cut short.
(Prov. 10:27)

But this was not true for Naboth (1 Kgs 21) or Stephen (Acts 7:54–60) or even Jesus (Luke 23:44–49). One might argue that we are to interpret the proverb in the light of the hope of eternal life. This is quite legitimate in the context of the whole Bible, but the proverb is intended to give a general principle that applies to life now.

One of the most common errors is to think of the proverbs as absolute truth rather than general statements of probable truth. They tend to speak in absolute terms – good and evil; wise and foolish. In an ultimate sense, this is correct, but it is not always reflected in our experience in this world. This is why the wisdom books of the Old Testament also include Job and Ecclesiastes. Job's comforters have a rigid view of the way the world works. The suffering of their friend is sure proof, in spite of all his protestations, that he is harbouring some secret sin. The rebuke of the Lord which comes at the end of the book should warn us against an over-rigid interpretation of the proverbs (Job 42:7–9).

Proverbs calls for righteous living. This will often lead to blessing, because our Creator knows how we are made and his rules give us the optimum opportunity to flourish. But in a fractured world, righteousness may well lead to pain and loss. In such circumstances, we are called to fear God, to do what is right and to leave the consequences to him. This explains why Proverbs, although a much-loved book, can also be badly misused by those who espouse the so-called prosperity gospel.* Understanding the book within its wider biblical context will show how erroneous this is.

When it comes to guidance, Proverbs will show us that the wise way is always the right way. It will shine a light on the path that we should take. It will often give us a helpful incentive to follow. But there is no guarantee of worldly success.

A final word

The Bible is a grace-centred book. It is animated by the gospel of Christ, and this is certainly true of the book of Proverbs. If our reading of Proverbs diminishes grace in any way, then we have misread the book.

Jesus is the ultimate wise man whose wisdom supersedes that of Solomon (Luke 11:29–32). His wisdom dazzled the teachers of the law when he was a child (Luke 2:41–50) and as a young rabbi (Mark 6:2). He is our wisdom: 'It is because of him that you are in Christ Jesus, who has become for us wisdom from God – that is, our righteousness, holiness and redemption' (1 Cor. 1:30).

The gospel is good news for bad people and wisdom for people who have made foolish decisions. Even Solomon failed to follow his own advice and his life ended in shipwreck (1 Kgs 11:1–25). On the cross, the ultimate wise man dies for fools who deserve to bear the consequences of their own foolishness.

And here is the final application to the subject of guidance. We all, from time to time, make foolish decisions. Sometimes they are errors of judgment. Sometimes they are just downright sinful. But even the most foolish decision will not derail God's purpose or extinguish God's grace. All our wisdom is found in Christ. He is the Pole Star and we are to fix our eyes on him:

---

* Prosperity theology is the belief that it is always God's plan that Christians should experience physical health and financial prosperity. If they fail to experience this, it is because of their lack of faith.

Therefore, since we are surrounded by such a great cloud of witnesses, let us throw off everything that hinders and the sin that so easily entangles. And let us run with perseverance the race marked out for us, fixing our eyes on Jesus, the pioneer and perfecter of faith. For the joy that was set before him he endured the cross, scorning its shame, and sat down at the right hand of the throne of God.
(Heb. 12:1–2)

God promises to give us wisdom: checklist

1 God guides us by giving us wisdom to make decisions that are pleasing to him.

2 Wisdom is knowledge rightly applied.

3 Reading and obeying the whole Bible will make us wise, but this is the particular promise of the book of Proverbs.

4 God's wisdom revealed in Proverbs covers every area of our lives, and it is offered to anyone who will seek it.

5 Wisdom begins with the fear of the Lord.

6 If we want wisdom, we must pray for it and seek it diligently.

7 We can find wisdom concerning any given subject by stringing together a series of proverbs that deal with that subject.

8 We should take our time and meditate on individual proverbs.

9 Remember that the proverbs reveal general truths which usually work out but are not cast-iron promises of temporal prosperity.

10 Remember that ultimate wisdom is found in Jesus, and when we have been foolish it is not the end. He came to redeem fools.

Questions

1 Read Proverbs 1:1–7. What does this tell us about the origin and benefits of wisdom?

2 Proverbs 3:11–12 encourages us to maintain a teachable spirit. What does this mean and why is it important?

3 Pick a subject and begin to assemble a series of proverbs on the theme. Try to synthesize them in five or six summary statements. You may want to do this using the proverbs about friendship found in the footnote.

4 What are the main lessons you have learned in this chapter? How should they affect the way you think about guidance?

6

What about . . . ?

It began at breakfast

We made the decision at breakfast in a well-known fast-food outlet.

I had been pastoring a church in Worcester for more than ten years. For most of that time, Peter had worked with me and we had formed a great team. But the church was growing, and we wanted to find a younger man to come on board and work with me as a co-pastor, with the idea that after a few years I would move on and he would become lead pastor.

The decision was made before breakfast was over and we began to consider the profile of the man we were looking for before sharing it with our fellow elders and the church as a whole.

I had taught Richard, and he was just the sort of man we wanted. If he had not just accepted a call to another church, we would have approached him.

I was due to chair a pastoral support meeting in Reading. As I walked from the station to the church where it was being held, I prayed, 'Lord, you know what we are thinking. Please lead us to a man like Richard. He is exactly the kind of guy we need.'

The prayer was pretty specific!

I arrived at the meeting. There were ten other pastors there. We began with prayer, and I was flabbergasted to hear the first man pray, 'Lord, we ask that you will be with Richard today. You know that he must be so gutted that the call has fallen through. Guide him and give him peace as he waits.'

To cut a long story short, Richard's call to another church had fallen through, and I was on the phone to him before the day was over. Before the year was out, he was in place as co-pastor. After three years I moved on, and the church has flourished under his ministry!

I guess we all have stories to tell of exceptional experiences of guidance.

Through compelling circumstances, powerful and overwhelming impressions or the unforeseen intervention of another person, we have found God guiding us in undeniable and unexpected ways. In my experience it is rare, unsought, and always needs to be tested, but it is undeniable

We have seen that God expects us to seek his will for our lives by a reasoned and prayerful engagement with Scripture in dependence on the Holy Spirit. However, there are other factors that we might add to the mix when it comes to guidance. In this chapter, we will explore some of them. In each case there is both a right and a wrong way to interpret these factors.

Should we dismiss these factors entirely?

Our approach should be more nuanced than straightforward dismissal. It is wrong to demand such things, and sometimes they can be misleading and even dangerous. We should not make guidance conditional on their reception. However, understood in the right way, they can become part of the process of decision-making. God is sovereign and he can intervene in remarkable ways when he wants to.

In this chapter we will consider:

1 Circumstances
2 Fleeces
3 Strong impressions
4 Advice

1 Circumstances: the prompts of providence

We know that God is in control of all the details of our lives – even the small things, like the hairs on our heads (Luke 12:7). He is actively working all things for our good (Rom. 8:28). This should make us humble as we consider the future. The Bible encourages us to make plans. Paul did both for the short term (Acts 20:16; 1 Cor. 4:19) and for the long term (Acts 18:21; 1 Cor. 16:5–7). But there is no room for the arrogance of heart that makes plans without consulting God and then invites him to bless them as an afterthought.

James warns us:

> Now listen, you who say, 'Today or tomorrow we will go to this or that city, spend a year there, carry on business and make money.' Why, you do not even know what will happen tomorrow. What is your life? You are a mist that appears for a little while and then vanishes. Instead, you ought to say, 'If it is the Lord's will, we will live and do this or that.' As it is, you boast in your arrogant schemes. All such boasting is evil. (James 4:13–16)

Nonetheless, if we are wise, we will factor in our circumstances when we make decisions. Looking at a situation in a sober and sensible way means reading providence as well as we are able.

Let me illustrate. I have to decide about taking a new job. What questions might I ask?

- Has God given me the gifts that would enable me to do this job to his glory?
- Is the salary sufficient to cover my needs as a single person, a married person or a person with a family?
- Has it come at the right time as far as schooling my kids or serving my church are concerned?[1]

You may think of a whole series of other potential circumstantial factors you might want to consider.

One important principle to consider is that of the open door. This is mentioned several times in the New Testament.[2] In each case it is the indication of an opportunity that has presented itself. It is usually associated with the advance of the gospel. 'But I will stay on at Ephesus until Pentecost, because a great door for effective work has opened to me, and there are many who oppose me' (1 Cor. 16:8–9).

On another occasion, Paul asked for prayer that such a gospel opportunity would present itself: 'And pray for us, too, that God may open a door for our message, so that we may proclaim the mystery of Christ, for which I am in chains' (Col. 4:3).

But we need to be a little careful here. Just because an opportunity presents itself, it does not mean that it is necessarily the right course of action. There may be other factors that cause us to pass on an opportunity. Indeed, Paul did this himself:

Now when I went to Troas to preach the gospel of Christ and found that the Lord had opened a door for me, I still had no peace of mind, because I did not find my brother Titus there. So, I said goodbye to them and went on to Macedonia. (2 Cor. 2:12–13)

The open door is not so much an infallible sign of guidance as an important factor to weigh in the balance before we reach a decision. Opportunities come as a result of God's sovereign direction. Utilizing them – going through the door – is often a wise decision. 'Be very careful, then, how you live – not as unwise but as wise, making the most of every opportunity, because the days are evil' (Eph. 5:15–16).

However, there are situations that arise in which circumstances may pull us one way, but clearer reflection alerts us to the fact that the course of action we are contemplating is against God's will. Jonah was running away from God. God had sent him east to Nineveh, but when he arrived at the docks it just so happened that there was a ship going in the opposite direction.

But Jonah ran away from the Lord and headed for Tarshish. He went down to Joppa, where he found a ship bound for that port. After paying the fare, he went aboard and sailed for Tarshish to flee from the Lord. (Jon. 1:3)

R. T. Kendall calls this 'the providence of sin'.[3] Jonah was determined to escape and, lo and behold, there was the ship to help him do it!

On the other side of the equation, the absence of an open door does not mean that an action should not be contemplated. There are situations in which circumstances seem to be adverse and we decide that the lack of opportunity means we should avoid all action. But it may be an excuse for laziness. Perhaps we should think about our circumstances in a more imaginative or courageous way.

The Covid-19 lockdowns presented huge challenges to evangelism. The doors were literally locked! We might have taken them as an invitation to missional hibernation. However, many Christians responded with creativity, vision and ingenuity. In many cases, the door was lifted off its hinges!

Our decisions must be driven by faith and the Bible, not by adverse circumstances. Many of the most courageous pioneer missionaries have refused to be deterred by adverse circumstances.

There are other pitfalls to avoid when we try to read divine providence. Sometimes we can get it completely wrong. Remember Job's comforters. They were convinced that Job's circumstances proved that he had sinned against God. They misread the situation completely (Job 1:21; 2:13), and at the end of the book God rebuked them 'because you have not spoken the truth about me' (Job 42:7).

Just because we get our guidance right, it does not mean that our circumstances will be pain free. God very clearly directed Paul to visit Macedonia during his second missionary journey. Read Acts 16 – 17 and you will discover that Paul had a tough time – he was beaten and imprisoned in Philippi, hounded out of Thessalonica and derided in Athens. When he arrived at Corinth he was at a low ebb: 'I came to you in weakness with great fear and trembling' (1 Cor. 2:3).

Did these painful circumstances mean that he had got his guidance wrong?

Absolutely not! Churches were established and the gospel flourished.

God never promised us an easy passage. We follow a crucified Saviour. And remember that God's purpose is not only to build the church, but also to transform us into the likeness of Christ.

We must be careful of putting too much emphasis on circumstances. God has not authorized us to make oracles out of events.

When we look back on the route God has led us, we can be confident. I married my wife in 1979. Can I say with certainty that she was the one God wanted me to marry? Any number of factors could have prevented us meeting, beginning a relationship and marrying. In his providence, God guided my feet and my heart to this woman. She was a single Christian woman, I was a single Christian man and we fell in love! That's enough to convince me as I look back that meeting and marrying her was God's will for my life. I wasn't sure when we started going out, but now I do know that she is the one!

2 Fleeces: wet and dry decisions

When I was a young Christian, it was quite common for Christians to talk about 'putting out a fleece'. This is a kind of circumstantial sign designed to give God the opportunity to make his will clear. Sometimes it can be relatively sensible. For example, 'I have applied for two jobs. If I get an offer from either of them, I'll go with the offer that comes first.'

This may be described as wisdom in disguise. Sometimes we are not seeking to test God but simply to set reasonable and measurable goals.

On other occasions it can be quite bizarre: 'If the next car I see from my window is red, I'll ask Sally out on a date.' (One of my friends actually adopted a similar dating strategy. It is a minor miracle that he is now happily married, but not to Sally!)

The principle is based on a misreading of the story of Gideon.

God told Gideon that he would defeat the Midianites (Judg. 6:12–16). He gave him a clear sign to encourage his faith (6:17–24). He also anointed him with the Holy Spirit (6:33–35). It was at this point that Gideon asked for a sign and, having received it, asked for a second one (6:36–40). It should be obvious that the fleece had nothing to do with guidance. God had already given clear instructions. Nor was it an attempt to be sure of what he was supposed to do. God had already given Gideon ample evidence of his will. This was not the act of a faith-filled man, but of a man who doubted God. God was incredibly gracious and patient with his servant, and Gideon knew it:

Then Gideon said to God, 'Do not be angry with me. Let me make just one more request. Allow me one more test with the fleece, but this time make the fleece dry and let the ground be covered with dew.' That night God did so. Only the fleece was dry; all the ground was covered with dew.
(Judg. 6:39–40)

The biggest danger of this approach is that it is an attempt to bypass the difficult business of thinking biblically. It wants a ready-made answer without the hard work. God is gracious, and he may protect us from making foolish decisions based on faulty methods. He does this for all his children – all of us get it wrong from time to time. But this is no excuse. If the process of guidance is designed to transform us, then we should be suspicious of shortcuts.

3 Strong impressions: God told me

Does the Holy Spirit speak to us today though hunches or impressions or gut feelings? We began to think about this in chapter 3. Let's take it a little further.

It seems to me that there are two extremes to be avoided. On the one hand, there is a view that is constantly looking for some form of supernatural prompting on every occasion that we face a decision. It uses a particular vocabulary: 'The Lord told me,' or, 'I was led by the Spirit to do this.' It seems to have a hotline to heaven and carries a sense of unassailable conviction. It is difficult to argue with someone who has heard directly from the Almighty!

On the other hand, there is a view of guidance that leaves no room for God to prompt us in a particular direction. It is suspicious of all talk concerning feelings or the conviction that comes though strong impressions. It pushes God far away from us and allows for little personal contact between God and our souls.

Where does the truth lie?

We need to be careful of the subjectivity of our emotions. Emotions are powerful things. In a moment we can be elated or devastated. We can fester in bitterness or jump for joy. Our emotions may be prompted by external circumstances or internal inclinations, or may even just come out of the blue. They are a natural part of our make-up as humans.

Jesus, the perfect human person, had a rich emotional life. He wept over the death of his friend Lazarus (John 11:35); he was angry with those who did not honour God or exploited others (Matt. 21:12–13; Mark 3:5). We are to love God with the totality of our being, and this must include our emotions.

However, we must never allow our emotions to disable our moral compass. Strong feelings are not from God if they prompt us to act against Scripture. The man is deluding himself who says, 'I know that breaking my marriage vows and beginning a new relationship is from God because it feels so right. I feel so good about it, it has to be God's gift.'

Our emotions are tied to our desires and needs, and we often have a strong inner compulsion for our needs to be met. All our needs are met in God. We should be suspicious of anything that drives us beyond him.

In his sovereignty, God might give a particularly strong prompt to take a certain course of action. God may give us a burden or a conviction that we should act in a particular way. The story about Richard at the head of this chapter is one such prompt. However, we should be clear that the Bible does not promise this form of guidance.

What about a subjective sense of inner peace? Some see this as an essential ingredient of guidance. It is like a train waiting in a station. The doors are closed, the engine is running, the driver is in place, but if there is no green light he does not move. We need the green light of inner peace if we are to step out. Without it we go nowhere.

They base their conviction on Colossians 3:15: 'Let the peace of Christ rule in your hearts, since as members of one body you were called to peace. And be thankful.' Inner peace is the green light.

Unfortunately, Colossians 3:15 has nothing to do with the inner peace that comes from a right decision! The context is a call for harmony in the church (3:12–14). The 'peace of Christ' is to act as an umpire or arbitrator in the conflicts that occur between Christians.

When we reach a decision, it is often after a period of strenuous deliberation. It is quite reasonable that we feel at peace at this point, and it might be God's encouragement because we know that we have decided according to his revealed will in Scripture. However, it is not promised or guaranteed. After his decision to preach in Corinth, Paul still felt weak and fearful (1 Cor. 2:3). Our hearts are deceitful, and we may have a sense of peace even when our decision is against God's will.

So how do we weigh our emotions?

We must not ignore them, but neither must we rely too heavily on them. We must be careful about the language we use. Claiming that an impulse or a gut feeling has the same status as Scripture or that it can trump every other consideration is arrogant and foolish. Like everything, we should test them by Scripture. In humility we should be open to the possibility that our feelings might be wrong. We can discuss our feelings with those from whom we seek counsel.

But having said all that, God knows us and calls us to delight in him, and promises that if we do so he will give us the desires of our hearts (Ps. 37:4). In his kindness, he may set his seal on a decision by granting a real sense that he is in it. A sense of unease should not be dismissed in a cavalier fashion. The default position is to settle matters in our minds (1 Cor. 7:37) and if, after much deliberation, we still feel unsure, it is best to stay put (1 Cor. 7:17–23)

4 Advice: two ears and one mouth

You probably know the old proverb, 'We have two ears and one mouth so that we can listen twice as much as we speak.'[4]

It is attributed to Epictetus, a Greek philosopher who served Emperor Nero in the first century. King Solomon was well aware of the principle a thousand years earlier. In the book of Proverbs, he enunciates it several times:

The way of a fool is right in his own eyes,
  but a wise man listens to advice.
(Prov. 12:15 ESV UK)

If one gives an answer before he hears,
    it is his folly and shame.
(Prov. 18:13 ESV UK)

Cease to hear instruction, my son,
    and you will stray from the words of knowledge.
(Prov. 19:27 ESV UK)

Where there is no guidance, a people falls,
    but in an abundance of counsellors there is safety.
(Prov. 11:14 ESV UK)

By insolence comes nothing but strife,
    but with those who take advice is wisdom.
(Prov. 13:10 ESV UK)

Listen to advice and accept instruction,
    that you may gain wisdom in the future.
(Prov. 19:20 ESV UK)

In the context of the book of Proverbs, this is a call to listen to the wisdom that Solomon has received from God. For us it means listening to Scripture and submitting all our plans and purposes to its direction. It is an affirmation of the central role of the Bible when it comes to guidance.

However, there is also a wider application. In our individualistic Western culture, we tend to think in very personalized terms. Instead of asking, What is right?' we ask, What is right for me?' And woe betide anyone who has the temerity to question our decisions. Biblical wisdom challenges this. Just read again the verses quoted above.

The Bible encourages us to make decisions in fellowship with others. Seeking the counsel of others requires humility. They may not agree with us! However, there can be wisdom in numbers. Moses' father-in-law gave him advice that may have saved his life (Exod. 18:17–23), and Paul gave very strong directional advice to the churches in Galatia – even when they did not ask for it (Gal. 1:6–10)!

Our faith is personal but never private. We can only work it out in the context of the local church. If we are joined to Christ, we are joined to his people. How will my decisions affect my church family?

Who do we listen to? Making the right choice here is important.

Solomon's son Rehoboam had to choose between the advice of his father's counsellors and that of the young men he had grown up with (1 Kgs 12:1–24). He chose wrongly, with disastrous consequences. We have to choose carefully. We should seek out those who are mature in the faith, who have a good grasp of the Bible and who know us and love us. This will usually be mature Christians and may include church leaders or others who have been on the road longer than we have.

Should we ask advice from non-Christians? That depends on the kind of advice we are looking for. Experts in a field may be very helpful. But we must remember that they have a world view and we need to filter what we hear. We should be careful of consulting too many people or of searching until we find someone who agrees with us. 'An honest answer is like a kiss on the lips' (Prov. 24:26).

Remember that seeking guidance is all part of the process of getting to know God and of being transformed to be like Christ. God uses the advice and direction of others to test out our motivation and sharpen us: 'As iron sharpens iron, so one person sharpens another' (Prov. 27:17).

Of the four factors discussed in this chapter, seeking godly counsel is the one that can lay most claim to being an important part of the process of decision-making. However once again there are pitfalls to avoid.

Christian counsel is directional. We are asking our friend to help us to think biblically. We want them to use Scripture and wisdom to indicate a specific path and call for commitment to it. However, we are responsible for our own decisions. I cannot excuse my foolish decisions because of the foolish advice I might have received.

There is also a danger in what is sometimes called 'heavy shepherding'. This is a form of psychological manipulation used by abusive cults. A relationship can easily become one of unhealthy dependence and abusive coercion. Our counsellors are there to help us make our own wise and godly decisions. They cannot demand blind obedience. We must never give our conscience to another person. Be careful.

Nor are we bound to take the advice that is given. The unanimous advice given to Paul was not to go to Jerusalem because arrest and imprisonment awaited him there (Acts 21:4, 10–12). But he felt compelled to go (Acts 20:22). He was not ignoring their advice – he believed what they said. But he had a fuller understanding of God's purposes, which involved being willing to suffer for the gospel.

The best advice will bring us back again and again to the Bible and help us to think how its instructions and principles should direct our steps.

Coming back to our main contention, God can intervene in remarkable ways when he wants to, but most decisions will involve the four principles we outlined in chapters 2 to 5. God has given us his Word and his Spirit to help us to exercise our minds in a godly and wise way. He may also use circumstances or people or strong impressions to shape our thinking. However, he has not promised any of these latter things. We should receive them with gratitude but not count on them.

Gerald Sittser summarizes it like this:

> And what is that will of God? Is it some specific, secret plan God has for us and wants us to spend days, weeks, even years discovering? Not at all. Rather it consists of a sober life, living in the power of the Holy Spirit, and offering praise and gratitude to God for his goodness. Paul's main concern is about how believers conduct themselves in ordinary life.[5]

Questions

1 In the light of James 4:13–16, should Christians make plans for the future? How do we avoid being presumptuous?
2 Does an open door guarantee success? What does success look like? What should we do when we face a closed door?

3 In what sense might a fleece be 'wisdom in disguise'? Are there circumstances when it might be appropriate to put out a fleece?
4 Should our emotions play any part in our decision-making?
5 What are the advantages of listening to the advice of others? What are the dangers of doing this?

7

Putting it all together

We have reflected on the four principles that help us to understand the way in which God guides us. We are now going to explore how we might put these into practice. As we try to put this together, I want to suggest seven steps:

1 Surrender
2 Pray
3 Search
4 Gather
5 Think
6 Talk
7 Decide

Step 1: surrender

The main contention of this book is that guidance is not just a matter of making a good decision – it is much more about knowing God and living a holy life that is pleasing to him. So the first step is to begin to think about our motives and the state of our hearts. Paul puts it like this:

> Therefore, I urge you, brothers and sisters, in view of God's mercy, to offer your bodies as a living sacrifice, holy and pleasing to God – this is your true and proper worship. Do not conform to the pattern of this world, but be transformed by the renewing of your mind. Then you will be able to test and approve what God's will is – his good, pleasing and perfect will. (Rom. 12:1–2)

'Worship' invades every corner of our lives as we offer ourselves to God as living sacrifices. In every decision I take I want to be holy and to please him, not myself. Hobbies and leisure; relationships and friendships; work and rest and play – all are to come under the lordship of Christ. Above everything else, I must seek his kingdom and righteousness (Matt. 6:33).

If I am honest, this is a constant battle. I am aware that I am torn between my devotion to Christ and my own desires and aspirations and ambitions. We never get beyond this battle. Lurking in our hearts is the pull towards sexual immorality, idolatry, anger and deception (Col. 3:5–11). We cannot remove these things from the equation entirely, but we can be aware of them and seek, with God's help, to replace them with Christlike characteristics:

> Therefore, as God's chosen people, holy and dearly loved, clothe yourselves with compassion, kindness, humility, gentleness and patience. Bear with each other and forgive one another if any of you has a grievance against someone. Forgive as the Lord forgave you. And over all these virtues put on love, which binds them all together in perfect unity.
> (Col. 3:12–14)

These verses are immediately relevant to the subject of guidance. They touch us at the point of motivation, which is what drives all our decisions. In our decisions we must be aware of being torn in two directions and deliberately choose to be single-minded – submitting our hearts to the Lord and seeking his will above our own.

Step 2: pray

Guidance is about relationship, and relationships depend on communication. God does not spoil his children – he wants us to ask for light on our path. As with all prayer, we need to be persistent. The promises of guidance are so clear that we can pray with confidence that God will answer us. However, God does not promise to give us specific answers. As we have seen, he may – through a special providence, for example – decide to do so. But this is his gift, and we cannot demand it.

In prayer, we are putting ourselves in a place of absolute dependence. Look at Psalm 5. Here David is praying for protection from his enemies. He is under great pressure, but he knows what to do,

> But I, by your great love,
>   can come into your house;
> in reverence I bow down
>   toward your holy temple.
> Lead me, LORD, in your righteousness
>   because of my enemies –
>   make your way straight before me.
> (Ps. 5:7–8)

David's response is to bring his situation to God and to ask for guidance through distressing circumstances. He is prompted by the assurance of God's covenant love and the access he has to God's presence. However, what dominates his thoughts is his desire for his decisions to conform to God's righteousness. His enemies are unrighteous – they are wicked and arrogant (vv. 4–5), deceitful (vv. 6, 9) and bloodthirsty (v. 6). By contrast, David wants to behave in a righteous way. He longs for God's deliverance and for God's guidance – but not at any cost. He is passionate about righteousness.

When we pray for guidance, we are praying for light on our path, but we are also praying that we will respond in a righteous and godly way to the direction in which God takes us.

So what do we pray for?

- We want our decisions to be moulded by a deep passion for God and his will.
- We should pray for illumination, so that we can understand God's will as it is revealed in Scripture.
- We may pray that if the decision is unwise, God will stop us from making it.

- We should also pray for wisdom so that we can make wise choices.
- We should pray that we might think straight and have a good grasp of the factors that will determine our decision.
- We can pray, 'Take my life and let it be consecrated Lord to thee'.[1]
- We can pray that he will help us to avoid resisting his will and doubting his care.
- Beyond this, we should pray that as we follow God's path we grow in our relationship with the Guide, no matter where he chooses to take us.

In prayer, we submit our hearts to God, recognizing that our heart is often a battlefield. Prayer becomes part of the battle as we pray against indwelling sin.

Step 3: search

We pray for wisdom, but we also seek wisdom in the place where it is to be found: in the Scriptures. The next stage is to begin to gather the scriptural data relevant to the decision we face. As we have seen, the Bible does not give us a blueprint for every single decision in our lives. It sets out guidelines which we can apply in a variety of situations.

Remember what we said about stringing the necklace in chapter 5. You might begin with some of the insights in the book of Proverbs and then look in the rest of the Bible to discover what it says about a particular subject. You will see this at work in the next section of the book. When we think about church or work or marriage, we want to be clear about basic Bible teaching on these subjects before we begin to consider particular decisions.

Perhaps a word of caution is necessary here. We want to gather as much biblical data as we can, but we must not allow an overload of research to paralyse us and prevent us deciding. Don't be intimidated into worrying that you may not have covered every base. Don't use a lack of comprehensiveness to become an excuse for inertia. Do as much study as you can and then trust God.

You are now ready to move on to step four.

Step 4: gather

At this stage we want to begin to draw together the information we have gleaned and move towards a wise and informed decision.

We need to gather as much information as we can about the subject we are considering. So, for example, if I am thinking about buying a house, I want to gather information about the financial implications of a move, the proximity to my church, the way in which the house would meet the needs of my family, and so on.

You have probably been doing this from the beginning, but by taking the first three steps you are now in a position to ask the right questions. The decisions where clear moral principles are involved are easy. But most decisions are not like that. Therefore, we need to find out as much as we can about the proposed course of action and the consequences that may follow.

Proverbs 18:17 states, 'In a lawsuit the first to speak seems right, until someone comes forward and cross-examines.'

There are always two sides to every situation. Wisdom demands that we listen to both sides. So, for example, in choosing to follow a particular career path, learn as much as you can about the pros and cons of the choices facing you. Use every legitimate means possible to help you to reach a wise decision. Take as much time as you need – don't allow yourself to be rushed.

Step 5: talk

At this stage, it is good to seek the advice of other people whom you trust. In big decisions it is always good to seek the wider perspective of people who know us and love us. They can help us to analyse what we have gleaned from the previous stages.

- They may ask questions about motivation and ambition.
- They can pray with us and for us.
- They can help us to have a more balanced biblical perspective. We may have missed some aspect of the Bible's teaching on a particular subject.
- They may point out factors we have forgotten.

- They may have information about the circumstances surrounding the decision we have to make.
- They may know us better than we know yourselves and be able to give a more objective steer as to the direction we should go.
- They may be able to help us to clarify our gifts and abilities.
- They may help us to think more clearly.
- They may ask the 'difficult' questions.

We may not want to hear these questions, but the wounds of a friend can be trusted (Prov. 27:6). It is always good to have a sounding board, but we have to be willing to listen. The Bible emphasizes the importance of a teachable spirit. Remember: 'Whoever loves discipline loves knowledge, but whoever hates correction is stupid' (Prov. 12:1).

Step 6: think

By now we have accumulated a great deal of data. We have talked with friends and heard their opinions. We are approaching the point where we have to make up our own minds. To do this we need to think clearly.

Rather than dulling the mind, Christian salvation involves the renewal of the mind:

Do not conform to the pattern of this world, but be transformed by the renewing of your mind. Then you will be able to test and approve what God's will is – his good, pleasing and perfect will. (Rom. 12:2)

The powerful preacher Martyn Lloyd-Jones wrote:

Looking back over my experience as a pastor for some thirty-four years I can testify without the slightest hesitation that the people I have found most frequently in trouble in their spiritual experience have been those who have lacked understanding. You cannot divorce these things. You will go wrong in the realms of practical living and experience if you do not have true understanding.[2]

In the Bible, faith is not credulity or superstition.

In some ways we are to be childlike – but we are never to be childish. One of the signs of spiritual growth is the maturing of the Christian mind. This is not so much about our IQ as about the way in which we combine our reason with our knowledge of God.

You now have a lot of data to hand – the results of your prayerful considerations, the biblical teaching, research surrounding the issue under consideration, self-examination and the advice of your friends. Now you need to gather it together and weigh it up with a combination of reason, faith and Spirit-inspired wisdom.

Step 7: decide

You have done everything you need to do to get to this point. You therefore have to draw the process to a close and do something!

It may help to draw up a series of pros and cons. Many decisions are neither right nor wrong – but they can be wise or unwise. It may be helpful to take all your facts and place them in two or more columns. When you do this, the way of wisdom is sometimes obvious. One column may vastly outweigh the other. The way seems clear. However, it may not be so clear cut, especially if you are deciding between two or more legitimate options.

The title of Kevin DeYoung's book on guidance points the way: *Just Do Something*.[3] We can overthink or overspiritualize a situation. There is a time for everything under heaven, and that includes deciding and acting on it (Eccl. 3:1).

Tim Challies writes:

> When we rule out what God has expressly forbidden, and when we have searched the Bible and prayed for wisdom, we are free to choose. This seems to be what is modelled for us in the New Testament. We do not find people desperately seeking God's will through dreams and visions (though occasionally God saw fit to use such miraculous means), but we see people making decisions based on what seemed good or best or necessary.[4]

Sometimes the decision may be to do nothing. That is a valid decision and is quite legitimate. However, the Bible warns us about the danger of being overcautious.

Don't procrastinate. Don't allow circumstances to force your hand. Decide; act on your decision; trust God.

So here are the steps. Let me conclude with three final provisos:

- Don't treat this in a mechanical way. Often the steps merge into one another. Sometimes you might want to pray with someone and seek advice right at the beginning of the process. They are just a suggestion of an order to follow. Find out what works for you. Don't become the slave of a process.
- Don't try to go through these steps for every minor decision you make each day. 'Shall I have tea or coffee at breakfast?' 'Shall I walk to work or catch the bus?' 'As I relax this evening, shall I watch the football on TV or read a novel?' Remember that God gives us liberty in many of the decisions we face and we do not need to torture ourselves by becoming anxious about small matters.
- Be prepared for God to break into the process at any point. As we have seen, he has not promised to give us any unusual providences or strong and overwhelming impressions or special words of direction, and we should not expect them. But he is at liberty to do so, and we should be alert to such things.

All these factors are underpinned by what the Bible calls 'wisdom'. In the next part of the book we will seek to apply these principles in three common areas of concern. But before we do that, here are a few more questions.

Questions

1 'Guidance is about relationship, and relationships depend on communication.' How should this affect the way we pray for guidance?

2 'Above all else, guard your heart, for everything you do flows from it' (Prov. 4:23). How do we guard our hearts? What are we guarding them from?

3 How does knowing God help us to make wise and courageous decisions?

4 Reread the quotation from Tim Challies. How should this help us to make decisions?

5 Think about a decision you are facing at the moment. As an exercise, try going through the seven steps suggested above. Did it make the process easier?

Part 2

PRACTISING THE PRINCIPLES

Sharkboy

Do you know who Sharkboy is?

I have to confess that I did not until a few months ago.

It was Moses, my four-year-old grandson, who introduced me to this mysterious character. I was looking after Moses and he came to show me a picture he had drawn.

'What do you think, Grandad?' he asked enthusiastically.

'It's great,' I replied, 'but what is it?'

With a mild look of shock at the inexplicable ignorance of his ageing grandfather he responded, somewhat disdainfully, 'It's Sharkboy, of course!'

His disdain deepened even further when I admitted that I had never heard of Sharkboy.

For the next hour I was educated in the wonders of this aquatic legend! I won't bother you with the details, but they were communicated by a very enthusiastic teacher.

During the next few days spent with Moses, I learned about all his favourite action heroes, marvelled at his dinosaur collection and discovered the joys of Top Trumps. I also had the chance to tell him some great Bible stories and to pray with him about some of the pressing concerns of a four-year-old.

Why did I spend time learning about strange aquatic superheroes and other arcane subjects? Because that's what grandads do. They delight in the things that delight their grandkids. Because I love Moses, I'm interested in the things that interest him. My interest is not confined to the things I consider to be important or the 'spiritual things' like prayer and Bible stories that are so important to me.

When it comes to my grandkids, there is no sacred–secular divide.

And there is no sacred–secular divide in the mind of God. Our gracious heavenly Father is concerned about every corner of our lives. We think that the 'religious stuff' is the bit that really matters to him. I may only spend a few hours at church each week, but this is of far greater interest to God than the forty hours I spend at the office or factory or school, or the hobbies I pursue or the relationships I cultivate.

Nothing could be further from the truth.

God is interested in the whole of our lives.

There are no corners of our existence that are private or insignificant.

In this section, we will try to put into practice the things we have been learning in Part 1.

We could pick a whole host of subjects to consider, but we will concentrate on three areas where Christians often seek guidance: church, work and marriage.

Each of the following three chapters follows the same pattern. In the first half of the chapter, we will explore what the Bible teaches about the subject under consideration. In the second half of the chapter, we will try to follow our seven-step model as we address the issue in hand.

8

Finding a spiritual home

God's view of the church

I had been a pastor for less than a year in a small church in Chippenham in North Wiltshire, when one Sunday morning two new couples turned up at the morning service.

This was a big deal for us. My wife and I were the youngest couple in the church, and we desperately needed an injection of youth and enthusiasm.

As soon as the service was over, I introduced myself and asked if they were from the area or just visiting. They told me that they lived in Cheltenham, some thirty miles away. 'We used to go to a church in Cheltenham, but God told us that it was not right. We have been looking for a good church for the last eighteen months. We have gone north as far as Birmingham and are now looking further south. But so far we have not found a good church worth joining.'

I don't know how long their odyssey lasted, but they never made a return visit!

I suspect that when they said they were looking for a good church, what they actually meant was that they were looking for the perfect church.

It does not exist.

But lots of very good churches do exist, and if you are a Christian you need to belong to one. I would go further than that – your Christian growth will be stunted if you do not meet regularly with fellow Christians in the context of the local church.

This is an issue facing all Christians, but it is particularly pertinent for students. Often they have come to faith during their time at university and have been nourished by a good Christian Union and a strong local church. Holidays may have been difficult, but they were temporary. But now they face the prospect of moving to a different area and are anxious about finding a good church.

We will begin by thinking about some of the things that the Bible tells us about the nature and function of the church.

What is a church and why do I need to belong to one?

The word church (*ecclesia*) is used more than a hundred times in the New Testament and it refers to a gathering of Christians.

The church is both visible and invisible.

In its visible and local form, it can take a variety of shapes. In the first century it appears that each city had only one church. The church owned no buildings that could accommodate large gatherings, so it was common for churches to meet in homes (Rom. 16:3–5; 1 Cor. 16:19; Col. 4:15). We do not know how these house churches related to the church in the city.

In its invisible or universal form, the church consists of all Christians from all times, whether in heaven or on earth, who are spiritually united to Christ as Saviour. Paul refers to this when he writes, 'And God placed all things under his feet and appointed him to be head over everything for the church' (Eph. 1:22).

John saw it in his visions on the island of Patmos:

After this I looked, and there before me was a great multitude that no one could count, from every nation, tribe, people and language, standing before the throne and before the Lamb. They were wearing white robes and were holding palm branches in their hands.
(Rev. 7:9)

The local church is a visible organization with traditions, a history and certain cultural manifestations. The universal church is invisible and consists of all Christians united to Christ and living under his lordship.

Every Christian is united to Christ by faith and is therefore, by definition, a member of the universal church. You joined the universal church when you became a Christian. You did not have to apply, and you cannot opt out. You are part of the 'body of Christ' (1 Cor. 12:27) of which Christ is the head (Eph. 4:15; 5:23).

However, you also need to be a member of a local church. The New Testament never envisages the possibility of a kind of freelance Christianity: 'I am part of the universal church; I don't need to express this by belonging to a local church.'

There are all sorts of reasons why people drop out of church attendance. Greater affluence gives us more options as to how we spend our time at the weekend. A plethora of activities are on offer for our kids, and blended and single families often mean that patterns of church attendance fall away. Lockdown during the Covid pandemic broke the habit of attendance for many people who replaced it with an online alternative. It is just so convenient to sit on your sofa drinking a cup of coffee as you participate or watch from a distance.

On top of this, our consumer-based society conditions us to think of church in terms of what it offers us. Like the couples at the beginning of this chapter, we become very picky. We say we are looking for the good when in fact we are searching for the perfect. When a particular church or series of churches disappoints us, we decide to opt out altogether. Do I really need the church to enable me to grow as a Christian? In an age of self-directed spirituality, we can access whatever we want remotely. Why go to the bother of joining a local church with all its hang-ups and imperfections?

As a Christian, I can only function properly and grow in a healthy way in the context of a local church. The writer to the Hebrews warns us:

And let us consider how we may spur one another on towards love and good deeds, not giving up meeting together, as some

are in the habit of doing, but encouraging one another – and all the more as you see the Day approaching.
(Heb. 10:24–25)

Encouragement has been described as 'the oxygen of the soul'.[1] Life is tough. The Christian life is demanding. Most of the people we meet every day need encouragement. We need to belong to a nurturing Christian community.

And what are we supposed to do when we attend church? Hebrews tells us that we are to go with a definite agenda. We are to consider our purpose for being there. We go to give, not just to get. We are to give encouragement, so that our fellow Christians feel affirmed in their faith and are inspired towards love and good deeds.

There is nothing more unchristian than a solitary Christian.

How do I know which is the right church to join?

In the first century there was no difficulty deciding because there was only one church to join! When there was a difference of opinion between different groups in the church in Jerusalem, they did not split and set up rival churches. They worked through their problems and expressed their unity (Acts 6:1–7).

Two thousand years later, things are different.

We are faced with a confusing plethora of denominations and parachurch organizations. There are Catholics, Protestants and Orthodox churches; there are Reformed and Pentecostal and Charismatic churches; there are Baptists and Brethren, Anglicans and Methodists, Independents Congregationalists and Evangelicals. And then there are churches that refuse to take any label. How do I find the right church? What should I look for? How do I know where God wants me to serve him?

As with so many questions of guidance, there is no single answer to this question. When you move to a new community and begin to look for a spiritual home, there may be several good churches for you to choose from where you could grow and flourish as a Christian.

Don't expect God to tell you the name of a specific church. As with so many other issues, do your research, visit several churches, talk to people you trust and ask their advice, and then decide. Once you have made your decision, stick to it!

Some people feel loyalty to a particular denomination or group. You might check out the churches from that denomination before you look elsewhere. However, you may discover that the local expression of a particular denomination may not fit the profile of a New Testament church and you may be compelled to look beyond it. As with all questions of guidance, everything has to be led by submission to biblical principles.

At this point, we can begin to work through our seven steps outlined in chapter seven.

Step 1: surrender

- What am I looking for in a church? Am I willing to find a church where I can serve God faithfully irrespective of its size or popularity?
- Am I open to becoming part of a struggling church where there is no room for passengers?
- Do I love the church as Jesus loves the church or do I have a critical spirit which will always see what is wrong with the church?
- Am I fully committed to the idea that the church is not there to serve me?
- Do I recognize that I need the church and I will never flourish if I stand aloof?

Step 2: pray

- Pray that God would guide you to a good church.
- Pray for discernment.
- Pray for wisdom to ask the right questions.
- Pray that you might find a spiritual home where you can be well taught, experience genuine fellowship and find an opportunity to serve.
- Pray that when you visit the church you might find a warm welcome.

Step 3: search

What biblical guideline does God give for finding a spiritual home?

You want to be confident that the church you join follows a New Testament pattern. Sadly, not all churches do. There are some issues that are so essential to a healthy church that their absence would cause you to strike that church off your list of potential spiritual homes. Then there are secondary issues in which good gospel churches take a different line. Some of these issues are matters of conscience and others are matters of taste.

I don't want to be over prescriptive, but here are some of the things to think about as you investigate a church:

- Are the people who form the core of the church Christians? This may sound an obvious question, but it still needs to be asked. Every vibrant church will welcome people who are not yet converted. Indeed, you should be suspicious of a church that does not make visitors welcome. However, the core of the church should be made up of those who have a living faith in Christ.
- Does the church honour the Bible as the Word of God and accept its truth and sufficiency and final authority?
- Is the church committed to the essential core doctrines taught in the Bible? Sound teaching is important. The Bible says, 'There is one body, and one Spirit, just as you were called to one hope when you were called; one Lord, one faith, one baptism; one God and Father of all, who is over all and through all and in all' (Eph. 4:4–6).
  - Do they believe in the Trinity – one God who exists in three co-equal and co-eternal Persons?
  - Do they believe in the full deity and humanity of Jesus – one Person with two natures?
  - Do they believe what the Bible teaches about Jesus – the virgin birth, his atoning sacrifice and his bodily resurrection?
  - Do they believe in justification by faith alone – we are saved by grace alone through faith alone in Christ alone?

- Are their moral and ethical teaching and practice in line with the teaching of the Bible?
- Is the church passionate about the great commission? Is it outward looking or does it have a maintenance mentality?

Step 4: gather

As you begin a church search, you will want to satisfy yourself that it is in harmony with the characteristics of a healthy church identified in the last section.

You may find that the first church you visit is the one where you settle. However, in most cases you may need to visit several churches before you decide. You can begin to gather information by looking on the website.

- Ask to see the church's doctrinal statement.
- Listen to the preaching – you can often hear sermons online. You may be able to watch the church's streamed worship.
- Check out the church's connections. Its 'links' will often indicate something of its character.
- What is the profile of the congregation? Is it a student church? Are there many families at the church? Is there a good cross-section of ages?
- Who are the leaders of the church?
- How does the church make decisions?
- What happens on a Sunday? What other meetings take place during the week?

Step 5: think

There are lots of wisdom questions you might ask:

- Where is the church? Can I walk to church? Could I take my non-Christian neighbour, or would it be too far to go?
- Is this a community of Christians who are endeavouring to live their lives according to the Bible and seeking to grow in their faith?

- Is this a church where I can grow, where I can be challenged and nurtured and where I can find a place to serve and minister to others?
- If you have family, you need to consider how your spouse and children would flourish in such a church.

Step 6: talk

- If you are moving to a new location, talk with people who know the area and may be able to give you a steer.
- Talk with the leaders of the church you currently attend. What advice can they give?
- Talk to the people at the church you are exploring. Perhaps you could talk with the pastor or one of the church leaders.
- Talk with your spouse and, depending on their age, your children. Would they grow as Christians in this church? Are there groups that would cater for their spiritual needs?

Step 7: decide

- Once you have decided on the church, get involved and throw yourself into the life of the fellowship. Churches have different ways of recognizing membership. Find out its practice and get stuck in!
- If one exists, commit to a small group where you can build relationships.
- Seek out opportunities to serve. What gifts do you have? How might they be used?
- Having committed to the church, you should stay there. In what circumstances is it right to leave a church? We will consider this later in the chapter.
- One last word – having joined a local church, you will soon find that it is far from perfect! Every visible and local church consists of a mixture of members, all of whom are flawed to one extent or another. Even though you will not find a perfect church, do your best to find a solid church that honours the Bible and the essential beliefs of Christianity.

When it is wrong to leave a church

When we are choosing a supermarket, we ask a series of questions about location, convenience and value. If you have to shop, you want the experience to be as positive as possible. Of course, these days they will deliver to your door, and you can bypass the whole hassle of shopping. Either way the key question is, 'What suits me best and gives me what I want?'

It is easy to apply this same test to the church. It exists for my convenience, and through the wonders of live streaming it can even deliver spirituality to my door.

The analogy may be suggestive, but it is also iniquitous.

Church does not exist for my convenience. Yes, I need to be part of it in order to flourish as a Christian, but growth comes through costly commitment and painful participation. The idea that I only stay with a church while it suits me and my family and I leave when a better option presents itself is unbiblical. It is also dangerous in the sense that it breeds a contempt for the church and a self-centred spirituality.

Of course, there may be a right time to move from one church to another, but often the desire to move on is driven by immaturity rather than principle.

Beware of itchy feet. Avoid the pull of the popular 'trending church'. Don't be driven by the fear that if I stay where I am I might miss out on the great things that God is doing elsewhere.

Many people do not leave a church for good reasons. Most of the time it is because they think that the church is not meeting their needs, expectations or preferences. Shopping for a better church needs to be resisted. When you move to a new area, give yourself a limited time to check out local churches. Then decide and stick to your decision. Remember that no church is perfect. Embrace imperfection. Hang in there. All churches have ups and downs. The closer you get, the more obvious the blemishes become. But you need to persevere and become part of the solution rather than part of the problem. Love the church for all its faults and foibles. Remember that Jesus loved it enough to die for it. So don't bad-mouth his bride!

Staying with the church through a difficult period is one of the ways in which God leads us on to maturity. Working through difficulties rather than running away is an important ingredient in spiritual growth. Before I think about changing church, I should perhaps think more about changing myself.

When it is right to leave a church

This does not mean that it is never right to leave a church and look for a new spiritual home.

This may simply be a matter of necessity. You have finished your study and are moving away from a university town where you have been part of a vibrant church where you have been nurtured. Or perhaps you are moving because of your job. When you consider employment, one of the first questions to ask should concern the availability of a good local church. As we consider guidance, we often look for the job and only then think about a church. My advice is to reverse this order. Before you apply for a job, do a church search. It is possible to follow promotion and end up in a spiritual wilderness.

There are other legitimate and practical reasons for changing church. Perhaps you live too far away to be involved in the life of the church. Perhaps a new church plant is beginning in your community and there is a challenge to get involved. Perhaps your circumstances have changed and you can no longer travel to the church.

Talk to the leaders and to your friends before making a final decision. Examine your heart and check out your motivation. Leave cleanly and kindly and don't separate yourself from healthy Christian friendships with those who remain. Don't demonize the church you have left. Don't leave one church without being clear where you will go. Don't stay disconnected. Church may be messy, but there is no alternative.

But there are reasons for leaving a church other than geographical relocation or practicality. A church may change, or you may discover something about the church which you did not perceive at first. You may discover that your church is no longer faithful to the teachings of the Bible. You may conclude that what is being taught from the pulpit or what is being practised in the pew is directly opposed to what the Bible says. Be careful. No church is completely right about everything, and it is right to distinguish a local church from the denomination it belongs to. Some Christians are convinced that it is right to stay and fight for the truth. Others conclude that they should leave.

It is misplaced loyalty to stay in a church where every week you hear the Christian message publicly denied.

Some churches become toxic. They do not deny any specific Christian truth, but those in the leadership become domineering and overbearing. The moment they begin to demand that you obey them rather than follow your conscience as it is informed by Scripture, you are right to begin to consider leaving the church. Examine your own heart. Some people struggle with any form of submission to authority. Is that you? If you discover that you are part of the awkward squad, repent and ask God to give you a humble heart. However, if the leadership of the church becomes manipulative and controlling, you may need to get out!

The danger in such circumstances is that you begin to drift. If you have been manipulated in the past, it might prove difficult to trust the leaders in a new church. Ask God to give you a thick skin and a tender heart. You need to be part of a church. Don't set the bar so high that no church could ever qualify. Don't become a spiritual nomad like the people at the beginning of this chapter. Learn to forgive. It is one of the hardest things God tells us to do. It is also one of the most fruitful. There is no future in bitterness.

Questions

1 Look at Hebrews 10:24–25. How could this be worked out in the life of a local church?
2 How do we cope with the discovery that the church we attend is imperfect?
3 Take a look at the letters to the seven churches in Revelation 2 – 3. What does Jesus commend? What does he condemn?
4 How has a 'consumer mentality' affected the way in which we think about the church and about the Christian life?

9

Work, rest and play

Just the job

A fellow pastor once told me about a member of his congregation who came to seek advice about applying for a particular job.

On the face of it there seemed to be a lot in favour of the job. He would be working for what looked like an honest company in an honourable profession. It offered a good salary and significant benefits. There were prospects of rapid promotion, and the demands of the job seemed to fit the man's skill set. On top of that he would not have to move and could continue serving as a Sunday School teacher in the church. They prayed together and the man sent in his application form.

Within a couple of days, the man phoned excitedly to say that he had been called to interview.

A couple of days after the interview my friend asked him how it had gone. 'Oh, it was perfect. It was all I had expected and more. And they offered it to me – but I turned it down!'

This seemed to be a strange decision, until the man explained that at the end of the interview, when they had told him that they wanted him to take the job, they added, 'You are just the kind of person we are looking for. The sky is the limit. All we ask is total commitment. If you join our company, your job has to become your god.'

They probably meant it as a figure of speech – but it was enough to convince him that this could not be God's will for him.

God is concerned about the job we do, and if we are serious about our faith, we will want to please him by the decisions we make concerning employment.

Your job is part of your calling.

Mark Greene quotes the comment of a teacher who spoke to him:

> I spend an hour a week teaching Sunday school and they haul
> me up to the front of the church and pray for me. The rest of the
> week I'm a full-time teacher and the church has never prayed
> for me.[1]

There is a tendency to think that church-paid ministry is a higher
calling than secular work. This is deeply rooted and hard to overturn.
However, it is entirely unbiblical. Every legitimate human endeavour
is of intrinsic worth. Even the most apparently mundane enterprise
can bring glory to God. In the Bible and in the mind of God there is
no sacred–secular divide. We sometimes think that some parts of
our lives – Sunday church, reading the Bible, witnessing to friends –
are important to God. The other bits – work, rest and play – are
beyond his concern. After all, he has a big universe to run – why
would he be interested in the minor details of my life?

Nothing could be further from the truth. All life is important to
God.

God is serious about the decisions we make concerning our work.

What does the Bible teach about work?

Work was ordained by God as a means of fulfilment, service and
worship. It is part of the normal routine of living. The Bible has a lot
to say about work. It begins by describing a God who works in creation and then rests as he enjoys contemplating the fruits of his
labours (Gen. 1:1 – 2:3).

This same God created human beings in his image, giving
them an important role in defending and caring for his creation
(Gen. 1:26–28; 2:15). Work is part of the created order (Ps. 104:23).
The Bible encourages us to work diligently and to avoid sloth
(Prov. 20:4, 13; 21:25–26; 26:13–16; 28:19).

Work has been affected by the Fall so that now it can become la-
borious toil (Gen. 3:17–19). Even the creation is subject to the 'bondage

of decay' (Rom. 8:20–21). Our work can be affected by sin and so become a vehicle for sinful actions (Amos 8:4–6; Jas 4:13–14).

The book of Ecclesiastes takes an honest and unvarnished look at the world of work. Because the world is broken, work can be frustrating, unsatisfying and wearisome:

> Yet when I surveyed all that my hands had done
>> and what I had toiled to achieve,
> everything was meaningless, a chasing after the wind;
>> nothing was gained under the sun.
> (Eccl. 2:11)

Like so many things, toil can appear to be pointless:

> What do people gain from all their labours
>> at which they toil under the sun? . . .
> All things are wearisome,
>> more than one can say.
> The eye never has enough of seeing,
>> nor the ear its fill of hearing.
> (Eccl. 1:3, 8)

However, the Teacher does not despair, for work remains one of God's good gifts:

> He has made everything beautiful in its time. He has also set eternity in the human heart; yet no one can fathom what God has done from beginning to end. I know that there is nothing better for people than to be happy and to do good while they live. That each of them may eat and drink, and find satisfaction in all their toil – this is the gift of God.
> (Eccl. 3:11–13)

We must never despise it, and in the Ten Commandments God commands both work and rest as part of the healthy pattern of our lives (Exod. 20:8–11). Heaven is described as a place of rest (Rev. 14:13).

However, it is also a place of 'curse-free' labour in a restored paradise: 'No longer will there be any curse. The throne of God and of the Lamb will be in the city, and his servants will serve him' (Rev. 22:3).

So work is not a distraction. It is part of what it means to be human and is an expression of being made in God's image. It is also our eternal destiny.

The Bible teaches too that God has established a pattern of work and rest within his world (Gen. 2:1–3). This is a pattern built into the creation (Ps. 104:19–23), and we are to follow this pattern – indeed, the Ten Commandments elevate rest to an obligation. So we should avoid laziness (Prov. 6:9–11; 10:4–5; 14:23), but we should also avoid overwork (Exod. 18:13–24; Luke 10:38–42). We rest because we need it and because we want to refocus our devotion on God. A weekly day of rest, refreshment and worship is a good gift from our Creator. When we rest, we recognize that we do not live by bread alone and that we are dependent on God (Deut. 8:3).

> In vain you rise early
>   and stay up late,
> toiling for food to eat –
>   for he grants sleep to those he loves.
> (Ps. 127:2)

Motives for work

The Bible gives us various reasons why we should find a job. Paul speaks about motivation for work in 2 Thessalonians.

> In the name of the Lord Jesus Christ, we command you, brothers and sisters, to keep away from every believer who is idle and disruptive and does not live according to the teaching you received from us. For you yourselves know how you ought to follow our example. We were not idle when we were with you, nor did we eat anyone's food without paying for it. On the contrary, we worked night and day, labouring and toiling so that we would not be a burden to any of you. We did this, not

because we do not have the right to such help, but in order to offer ourselves as a model for you to imitate. For even when we were with you, we gave you this rule: 'The one who is not willing to work shall not eat.'

We hear that some among you are idle and disruptive. They are not busy; they are busybodies. Such people we command and urge in the Lord Jesus Christ to settle down and earn the food they eat. And as for you, brothers and sisters, never tire of doing what is good.

(2 Thess. 3:6–13)

One of the great themes of Paul's two letters to the Thessalonians is the certainty of the return of Christ. By the time he wrote the second letter it appears that some people had taken this teaching about the imminence of Christ's return as an excuse for abandoning their secular work and throwing themselves on the charity of the church. Paul warns the Christians against such a person who is 'idle and disruptive and does not live according to the teaching you received from us'.

Paul could have asked for the support of the church, but he chose to support himself – presumably in the tentmaking business in which he had been trained (Acts 18:1–3). He encourages them to follow his example and work for their own upkeep.

People who deliberately set out to sponge off others are acting in a selfish and unloving way and should be avoided. Clearly Paul is not castigating those who want to work and cannot find a job. He is criticizing those who choose not to work as a lifestyle option. We should do everything to avoid becoming a burden to others.

The motive for work is quite clear here – it is the God-ordained way to survive in the world he has made. I am responsible for providing for myself and my dependants. I work so that I do not become a burden to other people (1 Thess. 4:11–12). God has ordained work so that we can be self-supporting (Ps. 128:2).

This seems very mundane and ordinary, but it is a fundamental motive for finding a job that will enable me to act in a responsible way. When it comes to guidance, one of the questions I should ask is, 'Will this job enable me to act in a reliable way towards those who depend on me?'

But there are other motives for finding work. One of the fruits of our labour is that it puts us in a position to serve others. So Paul writes, 'Anyone who has been stealing must steal no longer, but must work, doing something useful with their own hands, that they may have something to share with those in need' (Eph. 4:28).

Stealing arises out of selfishness, laziness and greed. It is to be replaced by honest labour which enables us to share with those in need. By finding a job that pays a salary that exceeds my personal needs, I am able to serve others. This is a great biblical principle. 'Therefore, as we have opportunity, let us do good to all people, especially to those who belong to the family of believers' (Gal. 6:10).

I am also contributing to the welfare of the society around me. This is true in a whole variety of areas. Teachers, shop workers, nurses, lorry drivers and so many more are performing acts of service.

Another reason for earning a salary that exceeds my personal needs is that I can invest in the kingdom of God. Paul commends the churches in Macedonia (Philippi and Thessalonica):

> In the midst of a very severe trial, their overflowing joy and their extreme poverty welled up in rich generosity. For I testify that they gave as much as they were able, and even beyond their ability. Entirely on their own, they urgently pleaded with us for the privilege of sharing in this service to the Lord's people.
> (2 Cor. 8:2–4)

Paul describes this giving as sowing gospel seed:

> Remember this: whoever sows sparingly will also reap sparingly, and whoever sows generously will also reap generously. Each of you should give what you have decided in your heart to give, not reluctantly or under compulsion, for God loves a cheerful giver.
> (2 Cor. 9:6–7)

Looking for a job that pays a good salary is not an end itself, and it can be a distraction if we want to indulge our own pleasures. But when I see it as an opportunity to serve people and to further the gospel, it is a worthy and valuable consideration.

Over and above all these legitimate motives, the Bible tells us that God has ordained work so that we can glorify God: 'And whatever you do, whether in word or deed, do it all in the name of the Lord Jesus, giving thanks to God the Father through him' (Col. 3:17). This applies to whatever legitimate job we pursue – from builder to brain surgeon and from politician to puppeteer.

> Obey them not only to win their favour when their eye is on you, but as slaves of Christ, doing the will of God from your heart. Serve wholeheartedly, as if you were serving the Lord, not people, because you know that the Lord will reward each one for whatever good they do, whether they are slave or free. (Eph. 6:6–8)

Choosing a job

Having examined the biblical principles, let's apply our seven steps.

Step 1: surrender

It is good to begin by thinking through my motivation.

- Am I driven by a desire for status and recognition? The Bible warns about this danger (Jas 1:9–10). It does not mean that we should never seek promotion, but we should be aware of our motivation.
- Am I motivated by a desire for money and wealth? This is another danger to avoid (1 Tim. 6:7–10). We cannot serve God and money (Matt. 6:24).
- Am I looking for another job just because I have itchy feet and am not content with my current situation? The Bible commends godliness with contentment (1 Tim. 6:6; Phil. 4:11)

and warns against seeking a change for the wrong motives
(1 Cor. 7:20–24).

- Will this job become an idol that demands things of me that
belong to God alone (Exod. 20:3–6)?
- Will this job be so demanding that it will prevent me from
being involved in gospel priorities? We are all involved in the
propagation of the gospel (Matt. 28:18–20; 1 Pet. 3:15). This
does not mean that I engage in verbal witness on the firm's
time. But am I able to do this job in such a way that I live out
the gospel in the workplace and people are prompted to ask me
about my faith at an appropriate time? Am I working in total
isolation, or do I have opportunities to meet with people I can
build a relationship with? Is the job so demanding that I have
no time or energy left to engage with church and use my
spiritual gifts for God's glory?

Step 2: pray

So what might you pray?

- You can pray that God will help you to find work so that you
can be obedient to the Scriptures.
- You can pray for help in the application process.
- You can pray that God will help you to think straight and to
follow the teaching of the Bible. If there are good biblical
grounds for not taking the job, the offer is a temptation to avoid
rather than a sign to follow.
- You can pray for honesty and integrity at the interview.
- You can pray for the wisdom to ask the right questions at the
interview.
- You can pray for pure motives and that, above everything else,
you will seek God's kingdom and his righteousness.
- You might pray for an open door. You may see the offer of the
job as a sign that God wants you to take it.
- As you pray, God may give you a sense of assurance about
a particular course of action, but as we have seen, he has not
promised to do this.

Step 3: search

What does the Bible tell us about selecting a job? The Bible will not name the company or direct you to a particular profession. But from what we have seen above, it is clear that we should seek a job that will enable us to provide for ourselves and anyone who is dependent on us.

There are many Bible verses I might consider as I seek work. Look at the following verses and explore how they might affect your choice of job:

Colossians 3:23: 'Whatever you do, work at it with all your heart, as working for the Lord, not for human masters.'

Can I do this job heartily to please God, not human beings? Am I driven by selfish ambition or the desire for position or power or possessions?

1 Corinthians 10:31: 'So whether you eat or drink or whatever you do, do it all for the glory of God.'

Can I do this for the glory of God? This does not mean that it has to be high profile or highly skilled – we can do the most menial tasks for God's glory. However, it is also obvious that some jobs would detract from God's glory rather than enhance it. For example, jobs that involve disobedience to God's revealed will would fall into this category.

Matthew 6:24: 'No one can serve two masters. Either you will hate the one and love the other, or you will be devoted to the one and despise the other. You cannot serve both God and Money.'

Are my motivations pure? Am I driven by a desire for money? Earning a good salary is not bad in itself, as we saw in the last section. However, when it is driven by greed, it becomes an unhealthy motive.

Ephesians 4:28: 'Anyone who has been stealing must steal no longer, but must work, doing something useful with their own hands, that they may have something to share with those in need.'

Is the job honest or does it involve me in actions that might offend my conscience or break God's law? Some jobs are inherently dishonest; others may demand behaviour that is deceitful or fraudulent. However, this will not apply to most jobs.

Colossians 3:22–24: 'Slaves, obey your earthly masters in everything; and do it, not only when their eye is on you and to curry their favour, but with sincerity of heart and reverence for the Lord. Whatever you do, work at it with all your heart, as working for the Lord, not for human masters, since you know that you will receive an inheritance from the Lord as a reward. It is the Lord Christ you are serving.'

I'm not a slave, but any job I take demands that I have the necessary skill set to do it well and with sincerity of heart. Do I have the right gifts and abilities to do this job? Is it the kind of job where I fear God and honour him?

2 Thessalonians 3:10: 'For even when we were with you, we gave you this rule: "The one who is not willing to work shall not eat."'

This is not an instruction for those who cannot find work, but for those who can work but choose not to. I may be struggling with my job and be tempted to resign and wait for something to come up. This verse clearly tells me that I should not do this. There may be moral or medical issues that lead to resignation, but I should not leave a job just because I find it difficult. There may be an occasion when I have to resign from my job, but generally speaking I should not do so unless I have somewhere to go so that I can continue to support myself and my dependants.

1 Thessalonians 4:11: 'And to make it your ambition to lead a quiet life: you should mind your own business and work with your hands, just as we told you.'

This is not a command to work with my hands – that is the cultural setting of the verse. Rather, will this job help me to work quietly and responsibly?

Galatians 6:10: 'Therefore, as we have opportunity, let us do good to all people, especially to those who belong to the family of believers.'

Will this job enable me to do good to everyone? Am I doing something that benefits people? Am I working in an environment where I can build personal relationships? Can I earn enough to supply my needs and then invest in gospel work or mercy ministries? By doing this job, am I contributing to the health of the surrounding community (Jer. 29:7)?

1 Timothy 5:8: 'Anyone who does not provide for their relatives, and especially for their own household, has denied the faith and is worse than an unbeliever.'

Will I earn enough in this job to enable me to provide for those who depend on me?

Hebrews 10:24–25: 'And let us consider how we may spur one another on towards love and good deeds, not giving up meeting together, as some are in the habit of doing, but encouraging one another – and all the more as you see the Day approaching.'

Will this job prevent me from meeting with God's people on a Sunday? We often look at salary, schools and neighbourhood before we take a job. But before these things, Christians need to be sure that they can find a church where they can serve God and grow as disciples. It is possible to find a great job but to end up in a spiritual wilderness.

There is plenty of data here to help us come to a decision. It will rule out certain jobs but leave others as genuine options. At this point, you are free to make a decision that conforms to Scripture.

Step 4: gather

In deciding about a job, you want to learn as much as you can about the working conditions and expectations. Use every legitimate means possible to help you to do this. Take as much time as you need – don't allow yourself to be rushed. But don't procrastinate either.

This will involve knowing yourself. We are all different. This is true of gifts and abilities. It is also true of temperament and character. You and I might go for the same demanding job. It may suit you because in the midst of stress you are able to produce your best work. What is more, your ability to flourish might bear testimony to the grace of God. But I might go under and not be able to cope. As I discover more about the job, my vanity might persuade me that I can handle the pressure. Knowing myself and my own limitations will help me to make a wise decision.

Part of your prayer and sober reflection is to ask God to help you to recognize your strengths and weaknesses, the particular areas of temptation to which you are susceptible, the way you will react in certain situations. All these things will affect your decisions.

Step 5: think

Begin to assemble your data. If you are applying for several jobs, you may want to work out a preferred order. You will also want to ask a series of questions at this point.

- Will this job put pressure on my marriage and family commitments?
- Will the working conditions make Sunday worship difficult? Some jobs, by their very nature, demand Sunday shifts. Think of nursing or policing, for example. It is right for Christians to serve in these professions, even if it might impinge on regular worship among God's people. Think carefully about this issue.
- Are there particular temptations associated with the job which cause me anxiety?
- If I have to change location, have I conducted my church search yet? Is there a church nearby that could become my spiritual home?
- How much of my time will be spent working from home? Will this suit me?
- Will I find time to 'recreate'? We are made in the image of a God who creates with infinite variety and beauty. Creativity is built into our DNA. But we all need to find the time and energy to do things that help us to relax and unstring the taut twine of our lives. We need regular stress busters.

- Will there be opportunities to build friendships with non-Christians or will I be working in isolation? Jesus was the friend of sinners. He flouted the accepted norms of the day in order to befriend them and create opportunities to bring them the good news. We are called to follow in his footsteps.

Step 6: talk

- Talk to the people who know you. If there is someone you work with, they may be of particular help, assuming they know you are looking for alternative employment!
- You might seek an objective view from a church leader.
- Talk to your spouse and family.

They may ask the 'difficult' questions:

- Is your temperament suited to this particular job?
- Will you need more training?
- How will it affect your home life?
- How will it affect your church life?
- Are there temptations that might be particular to you?
- Will you be in a situation of sexual temptation?

Step 7: decide

Having taken all the steps described above, you have to go ahead and decide. You need to go into an interview with a general sense that this job may cover all the bases described above. Something might happen in the interview which alarms you and changes your assessment. Pray for wisdom here – you might be asked to decide on the spot.

The Bible does not specify what job God wants you to do or for how long you should stay in that job. It does not tell you the name of the company you are to work for or the salary you are to settle for. That means that there are literally hundreds of different jobs in which you could serve God and bring him glory.

The Bible does not promise that when you have prayed and made your decision things will always be harmonious. You might later come to realize that the job was different from what you anticipated. You might discover things about your work environment or about your colleagues that make the job more difficult than you first imagined. It might mean that you will have to make moral choices which could lead to resignation or dismissal. This certainly was the experience of Joseph in Potiphar's household (Gen. 39).

Or you might find the work frustrating or boring. Ecclesiastes warns us about this. For many people, work is not a pleasure but a necessity. As a Christian, I do not find my ultimate fulfilment and identity in myself or my work. These things are found in Christ alone: 'Therefore, if anyone is in Christ, the new creation has come: the old has gone, the new is here!' (2 Cor. 5:17).

I have been adopted into God's family (John 1:12; Eph. 1:5); I belong to Christ and am precious to him (1 Pet. 2:9); I am God's temple where his Spirit dwells (1 Cor. 6:19–20). This does not mean that I should not seek a job that is more rewarding and satisfying. It does mean that I should avoid defining myself by what I do or romanticizing about the greenness of someone else's grass.

Questions

1 Look again at the quotation from Mark Greene. When was the last time you heard a sermon on work? Has anyone ever offered to pray for your workplace? Why do we continue to make the sacred–secular distinction?
2 What biblical advice would you give to someone who genuinely wants to work but is unable to find employment?
3 Look at the list of Bible verses on work. Which ones strike you as particularly significant?
4 How might our heart mislead us when we think about taking a particular job? Why are our motives so important? How can we check them out?

10

Tying the knot – or not

Questions, questions, questions

Choosing a spouse is probably the most important decision you will ever make. It is more important than your career or where you choose to worship. Marriage is a lifelong commitment which affects us, our families, our children and the health of our society.

And marriages fail.

According to the Office of National Statistics,[1] there were 107,599 divorces of opposite-sex couples in 2019, an increase of 18.4% from 90,871 in 2018. In 2019, the average (median) duration of marriage at the time of divorce was 12.3 years for opposite-sex couples, a small decrease from 12.5 years in the previous year.

As a pastor I have been asked a myriad questions about this subject:

- Should I get married in the first place?
- Does being single mean that I am missing God's best?
- Is it right to take practical steps to find a partner, or is this a lack of faith?
- Is it okay to marry someone who does not share my faith?
- Is sex before marriage off the agenda? If so, how can I know that we are compatible?
- Is there just one person out there who is the perfect partner for me – my soulmate? What if I miss them?
- If my marriage fails, is it because I got my guidance wrong?
- What do I do if the right person never comes along?

Marriage, sex and singleness

Since most of our guidance comes from the Bible, it will be necessary to begin with what it teaches about marriage, sex and singleness.

1 Marriage

In Genesis 1, God creates everything out of nothing by the power of his word for the purpose of his glory. As he steps back, he looks at what he has done and repeatedly declares that it is good (Genesis 1:4, 10, 12, 18, 21, 25, 31). When we move into Genesis 2, we find a single caveat to God's delight – it is good, except at one point: 'The LORD God said, "It is not good for the man to be alone. I will make a helper suitable for him"' (Gen. 2:18).

God therefore creates a suitable partner for the man (Gen. 2:20–22). The man and the women are similar but different – like looking at your reflection in a mirror. She is 'suitable' because she shares his humanity and they both bear the image of God (Gen. 1:27; 2:20). On the other hand, they are complementary beings – she is female, not male.

God now institutes the covenant of marriage. He defines it in specific and precise terms: 'That is why a man leaves his father and mother and is united to his wife, and they become one flesh' (Gen. 2:24).

Marriage is an exclusive, lifelong, covenantal relationship between one man and one woman (Rom. 7:2; 1 Cor. 7:2). I may cultivate a wide range of friendships and should not demand exclusivity from my friends. But I demand it and give it to my marital partner.

Marriage reflects a deeper and even more profound relationship – that between God and Israel (Ezek. 16:8–14; Hos. 2:7) and between Christ and his church (John 3:29; Eph. 5:25–33; Rev. 19:7–9). Contemplating marriage should deepen our understanding of God's love for his people, and exploring God's covenant love will give us a richer view of marriage. This is why faithfulness and fidelity are so important in marriage – it reflects God's faithfulness and the faithfulness he demands of his people (Isa. 54:5–6; 62:4–5).

In the Garden of Eden, the humans enjoyed an unblemished closeness with their Creator – they walked with him in the cool of the day. They also experienced a perfect relationship with each other, symbolized by the fact that they were naked and unashamed. Sin has disrupted this, but God's purpose in grace is to restore both the vertical and horizontal relationships which, as human beings, we ache for.

2 Sex

Sexual intimacy is confined to this exclusive lifelong relationship. Sexual intercourse is one of God's most precious gifts. The Song of Solomon is not a sex manual, but neither is it an esoteric allegory of pure non-physical love. It is a celebration of God's good gift of sex. The marriage bed should be both honoured and enjoyed and kept pure and protected from defilement (Heb. 13:4). God has set very clear boundaries which must not be breached.

After warning his son about the dangers of sexual sin in Proverbs 5:1–14, Solomon paints a glowing picture of the beauties of sexual love between a man and the wife of his youth.

> Drink water from your own cistern,
> running water from your own well.
> (Prov. 5:15)

> You are a garden fountain,
> a well of flowing water
> streaming down from Lebanon.
> (Song 4:15)

God is no prude! Sex is not tacky! Sexual intimacy is one of his best gifts. The first command given to Adam and Eve together was to have sex (Gen. 1:28), and Paul forbids abstinence except in unusual cases, and then only for a while (1 Cor. 7:1–7).

But sex is for marriage. Solomon continues:

> Should your springs overflow in the streets,
> your streams of water in the public squares?

Let them be yours alone,
 never to be shared with strangers.
(Prov. 5:16–17)

The streams of water are not for public consumption. They are to be confined to the marriage bed and not shared with strangers. This means that lust (virtual sex or pornography), fornication (sex before marriage), adultery (sex with someone who is married to another person), and same-sex intercourse are forbidden by God.

These are the words of a benevolent and loving Creator who wills what is best for his children. Human beings made in his image function best when they live according to his loving directions. The goldfish who wants to escape the confines of its bowl into the liberty of fresh air soon discovers that life outside its designed environment is no life at all. The same is true about sexual freedom and the restraints that God puts on it. Stay in the bowl!

3 Singleness

If marriage is God's wise provision for the enjoyment of sexual love, what do I do if I never experience such a relationship?

At any one time, probably around one-third of the adults who attend church are single. Some have been married and now experience the ongoing pain of separation, divorce or bereavement. Others have never been married and are quite happy and contented. Others have never been married and feel desperate about it. Still others are same-sex attracted and, as disciples of Jesus, are committed to a life of celibacy.

Singleness is not God's 'second best'. Jesus speaks of those to whom singleness is given – not as a judgment but as a gift (Matt. 19:11) and Paul also calls it a gift (1 Cor. 7:7). I do not think Paul means that some people have a particular ability to be happy in their singleness and celibacy. He is referring to the state of singleness itself. It does not mean that if at some time you choose to marry you are rejecting God's gift. At this current moment, the single state is God's gift, so enjoy the benefits that it brings. Trusting God means knowing that my current condition – single or married – is his gift for me, and I am to receive it with thanksgiving.

What are the advantages of singleness? Single people are spared the troubles that come with marriage (1 Cor. 7:28). Marriage is hard work. Sometimes it is a place of wonderful joy. At other times it is profoundly painful. No wonder Paul tells single people that he would like to spare them from this! And there is more. Single people can devote themselves fully to God's work:

> I would like you to be free from concern. An unmarried man is concerned about the Lord's affairs – how he can please the Lord. But a married man is concerned about the affairs of this world – how he can please his wife – and his interests are divided.
> (1 Cor. 7:32–34)

This does not mean that it is easy to be single. The New Testament is positive about singleness, but marriage is still the norm. Singles therefore have to struggle with loneliness and sexual temptation. We are not designed to be alone, and if we are single we therefore need to work hard at cultivating other relationships. The church should be a place where we are part of a family (Matt. 12:48–50), where we find many brothers and sisters, fathers and mothers and children (Matt. 19:29–30).

Neither singleness nor marriage is permanent (Mark 12:25). One day, Jesus the bridegroom will return for his bride. When that happens, all pain will be gone – the pain of a tough marriage or an excruciating bereavement or a difficult divorce or unwelcome singleness. All of us should keep our focus on this moment when disappointment will be a thing of the past.

Whether we are married or single, our ultimate delight is in God himself. We can never find final and full satisfaction in any person other than him.

Should I get married?

Christians are free to marry.

There have always been those who have taught that in some way it is more holy to abstain from marriage – as if celibacy is a higher calling than matrimony. Paul strongly rebukes such a view. Some false teachers will abandon the faith and follow deceiving spirits:

> They forbid people to marry and order them to abstain from certain foods, which God created to be received with thanksgiving by those who believe and who know the truth.
>
> For everything God created is good, and nothing is to be rejected if it is received with thanksgiving, because it is consecrated by the word of God and prayer.
> (1 Tim. 4:3–5)

God ordained marriage. As a Christian, I never need to ask whether it is right to get married. This is well within the boundaries of my Christian freedom. There are limits on who I can marry, as we shall see, but there should be no question about the legitimacy of marriage itself.

Christians are also free to decide to remain single.

I may remain single because I might never find someone I want to marry. Or I may deliberately choose to remain single. There are a variety of reasons why I might make this choice. I may decide that being single will give me greater opportunities to serve God. There are many pioneer missionaries who have made this decision. I may be same-sex attracted and feel that it is inappropriate to marry. I may suffer from a medical condition – physical or psychological – which would make marriage problematical. I might just decide that I would prefer to avoid the problems that Paul describes in 1 Corinthians 7.

Therefore, the decision to marry or not to marry is a question of Christian liberty.

On the other hand, it is perfectly natural and biblically legitimate to want to get married. So what can I do about it?

- Pray and tell God how you feel. Prayer is not a form of manipulation or a means of twisting God's arm. But I can tell God what is on my heart. James tells us that we have not because we ask not (Jas 4:2–3).
- Trust God to lead you. It is important to be patient and believe that God gives the best to those who leave the choice to him. Remember that the main contention of this book is that knowing the Guide is more important than knowing the way. Use the time of waiting to get to know God better.
- Use legitimate means to meet suitable partners. I grew up in an era of single-sex education. Churches often kept boys and girls apart. This may have seemed sensible at the time, but how will you find a potential Christian partner if you never meet?! It is important to find opportunities to meet other Christians. Sometimes friends may act as matchmakers. You may consider the careful use of a Christian dating service. None of these practical measures is a sign of desperation or a denial of the sovereignty of God.
- Date potential partners. If on the first date you announce that this may lead to marriage, it's unlikely that you will get a second date! However, dating should not merely be a form of recreation. You should not date someone who would be totally unsuitable as a marriage partner. Relationships can develop quickly, and you should be careful of hurting the other person. Remember that sex is to be confined to marriage and you should not experiment to discover whether there is 'chemistry' between you.
- Stop looking for the perfect person. He or she does not exist! Marriage is the union of two flawed people. This side of heaven you will not find anyone who is a perfect match for you. If you think that you are completely compatible in every way, marriage will soon disabuse you of this. Stop drawing up a profile and start praying to be the best husband or wife you can be. Become the right person rather than looking for the perfect person. Be honest about your faults and work hard at holiness (Phil. 2:12–13). Read God's profile of a husband and wife in Ephesians 5:21–33 and ask him to help you to begin to develop these character traits.

- Don't look for your 'soulmate'. There is a Hollywood myth that there is just one person out there who is perfectly designed for you. This is sometimes baptized by the church into the idea that, out of billions of potential partners on planet Earth, there is only one that you should marry. If you read the signs right, you will find that person and you will both live happily ever after. It sounds spiritual, but it is an illusion. If he wants you to marry, God has a partner for you. But he has not revealed his or her name and there are potentially myriads of partners with whom you could enjoy a wonderful, God-glorifying marriage. The danger with this kind of thinking is that you end up avoiding a good marriage because you are searching for this elusive person. The emphasis in the Bible lies elsewhere. Seek God's will, choose your love and then love your choice.

Is this a suitable partner?

The Bible does not reveal the name of the person I should marry, but it does give me some clear direction before I pop the question. Think about all that the Bible teaches and then let us apply our seven steps:

Step 1: surrender

- Ask yourself why you want to get married.
- If this relationship does not work out, will you be angry with God?
- Are you getting married because you are afraid of being left on the shelf?
- Do you want to get married to ensure financial security?
- Are you ready for marriage?
- Are you motivated by lust, or have you developed a genuine friendship?

Step 2: pray

- Pray that your motives are pure.
- Pray that you find the right person.
- Pray that you will be the right person – a godly husband or wife.
- Ask God for purity in the dating process.

- Ask forgiveness for past sexual sins – and then put the guilt and shame behind you.

Step 3: search

Work through the teaching of the Bible outlined above. Consider the boundaries – you are at liberty to marry anyone within certain biblical boundaries:

- You are only free to marry a member of the opposite sex. Marriage is the covenantal union of one man and one woman (Gen. 2:24). This is clearly countercultural, but as a Christian my conscience is bound by God's Word.
- You are not free to marry a close relative. The Bible spells this out in Leviticus 18:6–17. This is supported by UK law.
- If you are a Christian, you can only marry a fellow Christian (Mal. 2:11; 1 Cor. 7:39). You must marry 'in the Lord'. You are not to marry in the hope that the person may become a believer some time in the future.* In such circumstances, the couple will find that their values, goals and motivations are pulling them in different directions (2 Cor. 6:14–16).
- As a Christian, you should not marry a divorced person unless the divorce was on biblical grounds. Christians disagree about this, but my view is that the Bible does allow divorce and remarriage on the grounds of sexual immorality (Matt. 19:9) or desertion by an unbelieving spouse (1 Cor. 7:15). Of course, a widow or widower is allowed to remarry (Rom. 7:2).

Step 4: gather

There is no such thing as perfect compatibility, but there are areas you need to discuss in order to be sure that you can be of a common mind.

- How will you work out your relationship with your in-laws?
- Do you want children?

---

* However, if I became a Christian after getting married, I should stay with my non-Christian partner if this is his or her desire. If the unbelieving partner leaves, the remaining partner is not bound (1 Cor. 7:12–16).

- What are your views on parenting?
- What are your expectations concerning career?
- Where do you want to live?
- How will you handle money?
- How have you coped with disagreements?
- What are your views of church and Christian service?
- Does either of you have any desire to be involved in vocational Christian ministry?

Step 5: think

Use your God-given common sense.

- Am I friends with this person? Could I envisage spending the rest of my life with them?
- Sexual union is a vital part of marriage, so there must be at least some sexual chemistry between you. You are not at liberty to experiment before you are married – a truly special gift you can give your partner on your wedding day is the gift of your virginity. However, you should feel attracted to the person you propose to. It may sound noble to leave this out of the equation, but in the end it is foolishness.
- Having said this, the Bible puts greater emphasis on godliness than physical appearance. Attraction on its own is not enough. Human beauty will fade, but beauty of character will persevere. Make sure your hormones do not rule your choice. 'Charm is deceptive, and beauty is fleeting; but a woman who fears the LORD is to be praised' (Prov. 31:30).
- Can you pray together? Marriage is about companionship, and as a Christian you want a companion who shares your desire to love and serve Christ.

Step 6: talk

Talk to your friends and family.

- There is great wisdom in seeking the advice of the people whom you trust and who know you best. Your friends will see how you relate to one another and the way in which you deal with disagreements. They will be able to take a more objective view of your relationship than you are capable of doing.

- In particular, you should listen to the advice given by godly parents. This is not a deal breaker, because sometimes parents have mixed motives in the advice they give to their children. They are not necessarily objective in their assessments, but they do have a desire for your well-being and an inside track on your strengths and weaknesses. If they are alarmed, you should at least listen to their reasons for being concerned.
- In the Bible, the custom was for parents to choose a suitable marriage partner for their child (Gen. 21:21; 24:2–4). This did not mean that the couple was not consulted about the proposal (Gen. 24:57–58; 34:4, 8–9), and I am not suggesting that this would be an appropriate procedure in our culture. However, it does signal the fact that honouring our parents and listening to their wise advice is commended in the Bible, particularly in the book of Proverbs (1:8–9).

Step 7: decide

- Don't procrastinate. Marriage always involves an element of risk. I have prayed, I have checked the Bible, I have talked to my friends and family, I love this person and he or she appears to love me back. What more do I need? Nothing!
- If you are waiting for supernatural revelation, you will probably be waiting forever.
- There comes a time when it is cruel to keep someone waiting for the ideal circumstances. Trust that God knows best and step out in faith.
- Courtship is a bit like breathing. The Bible doesn't teach you how to do it. It just assumes you know. 'The way of a man with a young woman' is one of the things 'too amazing' for wise man Agur (Prov. 30:18–19).

- God is good, and he delights to give good gifts to his children.
  Falling in love is one of the most precious of these gifts.
  We should gladly receive his gifts, not doubting the goodness
  of our Father's heart.

Marriage is hard work – the myth of perfect compatibility is just
that, a myth. Marriage involves the death of our old way of life. We
are no longer single. We can no longer please ourselves. The goal of
my life is now to please another person. My dreams have to die so
that new dreams can come to birth. My ambitions and preferences
and passions must now be focused on the happiness of another
person.

A good marriage is not like a sculpture, which can be left. The
sculptor puts a cloth over his masterpiece and goes away. When he
returns and removes the cloth, it is as he left it. If you neglect the
masterpiece of your marriage, when you take the cloth away it will
not be as you left it.

Marriage is more like a well-watered and wonderfully attended
garden. It is the result of strenuous and exhausting labour. A
beautiful garden is the result of long hours of unseen toil. The
gardeners will have blisters on their fingers and aches in their bones.
What happens if they leave off their work for a while? The garden
will not be the same when they return. A neglected garden is overrun
with unwanted weeds. A neglected marriage will also descend into
decay and disruption. Marriages may be made in heaven, but the
maintenance of the masterpiece is down to us.

Questions

1 'That is why a man leaves his father and mother and is
  united to his wife, and they become one flesh' (Gen. 2:24).
  Look at God's blueprint for marriage. What does God tell
  us about the nature of marriage?
2 'God is for sex; sex is for marriage; marriage is for life.'[2]
  What are the implications of this statement?
  How would you answer the assertion that it is out of date
  and unnatural?

3 Make a list of the right and wrong reasons for getting married.
4 In the section on using our God-given common sense, there
   is a list of questions you might want to consider together
   with a potential spouse. What other areas might you want
   to cover?
5 How can I cope with disappointment if I long to marry but
   never find a suitable spouse? How can other Christians help
   with this disappointment?

Part 3

GOING BEYOND THE PRINCIPLES

Challenge

I became a Christian at a summer camp. It was 1967 and I was eleven years old. It was the cross of Christ that did it. As I came to see that Jesus had died for me, I fled to the cross and was filled with what the Bible describes as 'inexpressible and glorious joy' (1 Pet. 1:8). That same evening, I told the camp leader about what had happened, and he pointed me to Philippians 1:21. He said to me, 'Now you belong to Jesus. Paul says, "For to me, to live is Christ and to die is gain." That is your life now. Jesus saved you. You belong to him. Live the rest of your life for him.'

The statement made absolute sense to a newly converted eleven-year-old, and it still does! I did not understand all the implications – how could I? But today it seems to be one of the clearest summaries of the Christian life that the Bible gives us.

This is real, authentic and radical Christianity.

This is a book about guidance. Sometimes doing the right thing demands a willingness to make decisions that are neither 'safe' nor 'sensible'. There are ways in which making decisions is very similar for Christians and non-Christians. In both cases, we seek to gather all the information that we can and then run through the pros and cons. Perhaps we make two lists. In most circumstances, we will probably go with the list that seems most persuasive.

But that is where the similarity ends.

As a Christian, I may look at my list and everything might seem to suggest that the safest way lies in the direction where most of the factors point. But that is not where we end up. Sometimes we will make a decision that is anything but safe or sensible or 'reasonable'.

We may decide to act way beyond our comfort zone. Others may think we are crazy – including some of our fellow Christians. But what drives us is a passion to please Jesus and a willingness to see everything in the light of eternity. Far from being foolish or fanatical, we are living out the implications of our faith. We are exercising a wisdom that transcends mere common sense.

In this last section, we will explore the way God uses the process of guidance to deepen our relationship with him so that we come to rejoice in the wonder and beauty of our Guide. We will also affirm the faithfulness of our Guide. He will lead us to the end of the journey.

11

Knowing our Guide

Missionary to the cannibals

John Gibson Paton was born in Scotland on 24 May 1824. During his youth he felt called by God to take the gospel to the unreached people of the New Hebrides, the present-day Republic of Vanuatu.

The island was inhabited by cannibals, and two previous missionaries, John Williams and James Harris, had been killed and eaten in 1839. Despite this, Paton was determined to go.

When he shared his vision with the elders of his church, there was considerable opposition. One of them, a Mr Dickson, questioned whether this could be God's will. What if he faced the same fate as the previous missionaries?

Paton's response is touched with some humour, but it displays an understanding of God's will which is thoroughly biblical:

> Mr. Dickson, you are advanced in years now, and your own prospect is soon to be laid in the grave, there to be eaten by worms; I confess to you, that if I can but live and die serving and honouring the Lord Jesus, it will make no difference to me whether I am eaten by Cannibals or by worms; and in the Great Day my Resurrection body will rise as fair as yours in the likeness of our risen Redeemer.[1]

The hostility was not isolated:

> The opposition was so strong from nearly all, and many of them warm Christian friends. I was sorely tempted to question

whether I was carrying out the Divine will, or only some head-strong wish of my own. This also caused me much anxiety, and drove me close to God in prayer.[2]

Questions about guidance kindled a quest for a closer walk with God.

In 1858, Paton and his wife Mary landed on the island of Tanna and began working among cannibalistic tribes. Three months after their arrival, a son, Peter Robert, was born on 12 February 1859. But just nineteen days later, Mary died from tropical fever. Peter died a short time afterwards, just thirty-six days old.

Paton buried his wife and child together. 'Let those who have ever passed through any similar darkness as of midnight feel for me; as for all others, it would be more than vain to try to paint my sorrows.'[3]

Paton spent nights sleeping on their grave to protect them from the local cannibals. He continued with his work, but faced increasing animosity, with several attempts on his life. On one occasion he had to hide in a tree as his enemies searched for him:

I climbed into the tree and was left there alone in the bush. The hours I spent there live all before me as if it were but of yesterday. I heard the frequent discharging of muskets, and the yells of the Savages.[4]

Had he got his guidance wrong? Had Mr Dickson been right to be cautious? As he reflected on these painful experiences, Paton came to see the hand of God in them. In particular, he wrote of the deepening fellowship which he enjoyed:

Yet I sat there among the branches, as safe as in the arms of Jesus. Never, in all my sorrows, did my Lord draw nearer to me, and speak more soothingly in my soul, than when the moon-light flickered among those chestnut leaves, and the night air played on my throbbing brow, as I told all my heart to Jesus. Alone, yet not alone! If it be to glorify my God, I will not grudge to spend many nights alone in such a tree, to feel again my

Saviour's spiritual presence, to enjoy His consoling fellowship. If thus thrown back upon your own soul, alone, all alone, in the midnight, in the bush, in the very embrace of death itself, have you a Friend that will not fail you then?[5]

After many years of painful and self-sacrificing labour, Paton began to see fruit. Multitudes of the people destroyed their idols, and Christianity gained a permanent foothold on the island.

The central theme

This is a book about guidance. We want to discern and follow God's will. But there is something more important than seeking guidance – the overwhelming goal of our lives is to know the Guide.

We need to remember this when the process of guidance seems complicated and confusing, or when we make a decision that has unforeseen and painful consequences. At such times we need to stand back and see the big picture. The purposes of God focus on relationships. The way may be difficult so that I will lean on the Guide and find comfort and strength in him.

Knowing God is the central theme of the Bible. It is where the Bible begins. God created men and women in his image so that they could enjoy a relationship with him. Adam and Eve walked with God in the cool of the day (Gen. 3:8) – a picture of intimate and warm communion. Sin disrupts this relationship. If the essence of life is fellowship with God, then the nature of death is to be cut off from this life. Without God we are like a flower cut from the stem – we may appear to flourish for a while, but we soon wither and shrivel.

The fact that God comes looking for Adam and Eve shows that the Gardener has not abandoned the garden. He reaches out to them and promises a restored relationship. Through Christ this relationship is re-established, and the essence of eternal life is to know him: 'Now this is eternal life: that they know you, the only true God, and Jesus Christ, whom you have sent' (John 17:3)

To restore this relationship, God was willing to send his Son to the horrors of Calvary. The cross is the cost of intimacy with God. Every time I pray, I need to remember how much it cost my Saviour to make this possible.

The final outcome of this is seen in the last chapter of the Bible:

> No longer will there be any curse. The throne of God and of the Lamb will be in the city, and his servants will serve him. They will see his face, and his name will be on their foreheads. There will be no more night. They will not need the light of a lamp or the light of the sun, for the Lord God will give them light. And they will reign for ever and ever.
> (Rev. 22:3–5)

If life is a journey and guidance is about finding the right way, then this is the end of the journey. The purpose of the journey is to enjoy our daily walk with God.

Let Jim Packer summarize for us:

> We were made to know God. Our purpose in life is to know God. The eternal life that Jesus gives is true knowledge of God. The best thing in life, which brings more joy, delight, and contentment, than anything else is the true and saving knowledge of God. God himself desires that we would know him.[6]

A worthy ambition

Ambition may be defined as the eager and strong desire to achieve something. In Philippians 3:10–11, Paul shares his most intimate ambitions: 'I want to know Christ – yes, to know the power of his resurrection and participation in his sufferings, becoming like him in his death, and so, somehow, attaining to the resurrection from the dead.'

He knows Christ – he wants to know him more. He also wants to experience the life-transforming power of Christ's resurrection at work in his life. The gravity of sin constantly pulls us downwards, but Christ releases the gravity-defying power of the resurrection in the life of those who trust him. Beyond this, Paul wants to experience the fellowship of Christ's suffering. The word 'fellowship' carries the idea of partnership in the pursuit of a common goal (Philippians 1:5, 7; 2:1). We follow a crucified Saviour and are committed to his mission in the world. Paul's ambition is to partner with Christ in this mission, whatever the cost.

How could this affect the decisions we face? It inspires a series of questions:

- If my decisions are shaped by my ambitions, are my ambitions in line with God's pleasure and plans?
- Do I long to know Christ in a richer and fuller way?
- Does the upper thrust of resurrection power charge the way I think and the things I delight in?
- As I face conflicting options, am I willing to take a route which might lead to suffering because my first concern is Christ and his kingdom?
- Are my decisions short-term solutions to immediate problems, or do they always have an eye on eternity and the prize of knowing Christ?

A work in progress

Paul immediately begins to explain how this works out in practice in his life:

> Not that I have already obtained all this, or have already arrived at my goal, but I press on to take hold of that for which Christ Jesus took hold of me. Brothers and sisters, I do not consider myself yet to have taken hold of it. But one thing I do: forgetting what is behind and straining towards what is ahead, I press on towards the goal to win the prize for which God has called me heavenwards in Christ Jesus.
> (Phil. 3:12–14)

Growing in in the knowledge of God is a lifelong process. Christianity is a long obedience in the same direction. So every day, as we face decisions great and small, we have to recognize that we have not yet arrived – we are a work in progress. Paul's holy ambition (3:10–11) is matched by an honest confession and a humble commitment (3:12–14).

After thirty years of following Jesus, Paul is aware that he still has a long way to go. Every day we have to make decisions that will honour God and not ourselves. The fact that I made a godly decision yesterday is no guarantee that I will do the same today. The process of decision-making is supposed to challenge us and refine our desires. However much it costs, we must press on to seize the prize, like the runner who keeps his eye on the crown or the hunter who assiduously tracks down his prey (3:12). We must be single-minded and wholehearted (3:13). There are no shortcuts and no easy three steps to follow. There is no second blessing that raises us above the strife. We are to work out our salvation with fear and trembling (Phil. 2:12–13). Rather than letting go and letting God, we are to trust God and keep going.

Why is guidance such an important subject? Why do we often find it confusing or mesmerizing? The answer is that sometimes we forget that following Jesus involves negotiating difficult terrain. We live in a battle zone, and the battle is both within and without. Making godly decisions will focus my attention on what is really important to me.

What is the final goal? Paul tells us later in chapter 3:

> But our citizenship is in heaven. And we eagerly await a Saviour from there, the Lord Jesus Christ, who, by the power that enables him to bring everything under his control, will transform our lowly bodies so that they will be like his glorious body. (Phil. 3:20–21)

As a Christian, I am looking for the return of the king, for the restoration of creation and the transformation of this feeble body. Paul knew that after death he would be with Christ, which was far better

(Phil. 1:21–24). While the body sleeps, the soul enjoys the bliss of fellowship with Christ. This is the essence of eternal life. However, this is not the final state. There is a life after the life after death. This fullness of life begins when this lowly body is transformed to become like his glorious body.

This means that the decisions I make now should be animated by these expectations. Heavenly rewards should control my choices rather than the glittering prizes this world has to offer. Jesus warned us:

> Do not store up for yourselves treasures on earth, where moths and vermin destroy, and where thieves break in and steal. But store up for yourselves treasures in heaven, where moths and vermin do not destroy, and where thieves do not break in and steal. For where your treasure is, there your heart will be also.
> (Matt. 6:19–21)

In the light of this, Paul's final word is one of encouragement: 'Therefore, my brothers and sisters, you whom I love and long for, my joy and crown, stand firm in the Lord in this way, dear friends!' (Phil. 4:1).

A couple of years ago, my wife's sister took her on a two-week cruise to celebrate a significant birthday. I was delighted for her. The only drawback was that we were unable to speak. We exchanged texts, but for two weeks I did not hear her voice.

The first week was okay. I was busy and time went quickly. But by week two I began to miss her. Boy, did I miss her! I couldn't wait for her return. Love hurts. Solomon describes it like this:

> Place me like a seal over your heart,
>   like a seal on your arm;
> for love is as strong as death,
>   its jealousy unyielding as the grave.
> It burns like blazing fire,
>   like a mighty flame.

Many waters cannot quench love;
    rivers cannot sweep it away.
If one were to give
    all the wealth of one's house for love,
    it would be utterly scorned.
(Song 8:6–7)

After we had been reunited, I reflected on my emotions. I had been yearning to see her face and hear her voice.

In the process of us seeking guidance, God's overarching purpose is to awaken our hearts to yearn for him. He may hide his face and his voice may on occasion seem faint, but at such times he becomes the desire of our heart.

Isaiah 26:8 reads:

Yes, LORD, walking in the way of your laws,
    we wait for you;
your name and renown
    are the desire of our hearts.

Commenting on the phrase in the second part of the verse, John Piper writes:

Nothing is more important in your life than . . . the triumph of this desire over all other desires. If the name and fame of Jesus, the Savior, the Son of God, the King of kings, does not become your greatest desire, you will not only waste your life; you will lose it . . . But if Jesus becomes your greatest desire – though it may cost you your life – you will finish the race, take many with you, and together you will enter the joy of your master, forever.[7]

When we struggle with guidance, or when our way is difficult and brings us to a place of pain, or when our earthly comforts disappear, it is because God is seeking to ignite a yearning in our hearts which only he can satisfy. Anxiety about the future can lead to restlessness.

As our relationship with our Guide deepens, so these anxieties come into perspective. And, as Augustine reminds us in the opening paragraph of his *Confessions*, we find rest for our souls: 'You have made us, O Lord, for Yourself, and our heart is restless until it rests in You.[8]

Questions

1 'Lord, please may my life be shaped by the privilege of sharing in your suffering.' What are the implications of this prayer for the subject of guidance?

2 How can we know that our ambitions are pleasing to God? Is it right for a Christian to have any ambitions that are not specifically related to Christ and his kingdom?

3 How do I make sure that I listen to beneficial voices and avoid dangerous voices?

4 'But our citizenship is in heaven. And we eagerly await a Saviour from there, the Lord Jesus Christ, who, by the power that enables him to bring everything under his control, will transform our lowly bodies so that they will be like his glorious body' (Phil. 3:20–21). What impact should this verse have on the choices I make and the decisions I come to?

12

Trusting our Guide

The greatest generation

My mum was part of the 'greatest generation'.

The term was popularized by the title of a 1998 book by American journalist Tom Brokaw.[1] He applied it to Americans who came out of the Great Depression and fought in the Second World War or held their ground on the home front. They fought not for fame or recognition, but because it was 'the right thing to do'.

A BBC series and a book which grew out of the series applied the phrase to the UK:

> Although a few of the people who appear in these pages are better known than others, the majority bear only the distinction of living through, and responding to, the most extraordinary of times. They represent the generation born roughly between 1915 and 1925, who endured much, experienced much and built much of the world we know today.[2]

My mum lived through the blitz in Birmingham and nursed her dad, who carried a shrapnel wound from the First World War. She drove a delivery van and cared for younger siblings. Old and fading photos always show her with a smile, which masked the seriousness and anguish of the times.

When I was ten, I had to do a school project on the Second World War. I interviewed my mum and was amazed at the stories she told me. At that stage, Mum was not a religious woman and as a family we had no connections with the church. But I had started going to a midweek club at a little church a few doors down from our home in south Birmingham. I was interested in how people had reacted when bombs fell and demolished buildings they had grown up with.

'Were you afraid, Mum?'

'Yes. Every day. Especially at night when the bombers came. You never knew if you would see the morning. My parents would whisper about who had been hit. They thought I could not hear them, but I could.'

'Did you pray?'

At that point, Mum looked at me with incredulity, as if it was the most ridiculous question she had ever heard.

'Of course we prayed! I never went to church, but I prayed every night, and every morning I thanked God that I was still alive! I was sure that someone was watching over me.'

There is something written into our DNA that causes us to reach out to God when we are in extremis. I have met many people who have shared this sense of God's watchful eye in times of difficulty. Some might term it as weakness or superstition. My mum was a strong and very down-to-earth person. To her it seemed logical and practical to reach out to God when there was no one else to reach out to. God is not so much a crutch to lean on as a total life support system. Amid the uncertainties and ambiguities of life, we desperately need solid ground. And we know it. Without God there is no plot or purpose in our lives, the universe is indifferent, and life is a cruel tragedy.

We have seen that guidance is much more than just making good decisions. The choices we make flow from our relationship with God. They test that relationship and are one of the principal ways in which God transforms us into the likeness of his Son. They teach us to trust God and they deepen our appreciation of the Bible and of our Christian brothers and sisters. In his wisdom, God allows us to make decisions which, on reflection, we may have done differently. But when that happens, we learn so much from our 'mistakes'. God has not revealed the detailed blueprint we might crave, but he has made promises that we can count on.

And over it all, we can be assured that God is watching over our paths and leading us safely home. This is the theme of Psalm 121.

God is my strength – he never fails

Psalm 121 speaks of a God who watches over his pilgrim people. The Psalm describes the experience of a pilgrim as he journeys through bandit country on his way to worship God in the temple in Jerusalem.

The Psalm consists of four short stanzas and is designed to evoke faith and deepen trust, so that we make our decisions without fear. We can have confidence in the God who watches over us.

He begins with a question and an answer:

> I lift up my eyes to the mountains –
> where does my help come from?
> My help comes from the LORD,
> the Maker of heaven and earth.
> (Ps. 121:1–2)

The mountains mark the pilgrim's route towards Jerusalem. It is a long, weary and dangerous journey. Maybe the hills are an inspiring emblem of God's reliability and unchanging character. At the end of a turbulent life, David describes God in this way:

> The LORD is my rock, my fortress and my deliverer;
> my God is my rock, in whom I take refuge,
> my shield and the horn of my salvation,
> my stronghold.
> (Ps. 18:2)

This may be what is in the mind of the pilgrim in Psalm 121. However, it seems to me to be more likely that he sees the mountains as a sign of menace and foreboding. Bandits and wild animals lurked in their shadows and threatened his journey. That was why most pilgrims travelled in caravans and employed bodyguards to watch over them. But are the precautions sufficient? This is what prompts his question, 'where does my help come from?'

On our journey to heaven, we are faced with trials at every turn. We make our decisions, but who is there to protect us and watch over us? Who will keep us safe? To whom can we turn when the way seems torturous and long? If we are honest, there are times when circumstances seem to overwhelm us, and it feels as if life is like a dream – vivid and yet ephemeral. We are like a brief candle or a walking shadow.[3] Do my decisions really matter? What if I make a wrong turn?

The psalmist gives an unequivocal answer:

> My help comes from the LORD,
>   the Maker of heaven and earth.

We cannot turn to ourselves and our own resources. We need God like a fish needs water or like our lungs need oxygen. The psalmist describes God as both infinitely powerful and intimately personal.

On the one hand he is the Maker of heaven and earth. The mountains are dwarfed by their Creator. Everything that exists owes its origin and its continued existence to him. Mountains and oceans; giant redwoods and rhinos; Mount Everest and the Everglades; the Great Barrier Reef and the Matterhorn; the Milky Way and microbes; gorillas and goldfish; subatomic particles and spinning galaxies. Everything is held in existence by God. Next time you watch a breathtaking nature documentary, turn off the commentary and play 'How Great Thou Art' as a backing track.

God's power means that we will never face anything that is too big for him or which will leave him puzzled and nonplussed in any way. If peace is the conscious possession of adequate resources, then God is the source of peace, because his resources are infinite.

But, on the other hand, he is also intimately personal. He is the Lord who has revealed his name to his people. The psalmist knows that help is sure because he knows God's name. The name 'LORD' is a translation of God's covenant name, *Yahweh*. It is the name revealed at the burning bush (Exod. 3:13–14). When God gives us his name, he gives us himself. We are his and he is ours for ever and for ever. To know his name is therefore to know him and to be assured of his commitment to us.

> The LORD is a refuge for the oppressed,
>   a stronghold in times of trouble.
> Those who know your name trust in you,
>   for you, LORD, have never forsaken those who seek you.
> (Ps. 9:9–10)

With the coming of Christ, the ultimate has become intimate, and our knowledge of God is deeper through the knowledge of Christ. We can call on his name and know that he will hear.

Think about how this applies to guidance. It removes all the anxiety we might feel. God's resources are immeasurable. We step out in faith, knowing that all we need is found in him. But we also have confidence in him, because he has promised to be unconditionally committed to us. He will never break his promises.

What if I make a mistake? What if I get guidance wrong? We can trust God to shape all our decisions, even the bad ones, to make us like Christ. He is the potter and we are the clay. The trials of life are in the hands of the potter.

This is not an excuse for making irresponsible decisions. We have to live with the painful consequences of such decisions. It does mean, though, that in all circumstances I can trust God to work all things for my good. My irresponsibility will not sever me from his love.

The first question posed by the Heidelberg Catechism is, 'What is your only comfort in life and in death?' The answer gives us confidence in all the vicissitudes of life:

> That I, with body and soul, both in life and in death, am not my own, but belong to my faithful Savior Jesus Christ, who with His precious blood has fully satisfied for all my sins, and redeemed me from all the power of the devil; and so preserves me, that without the will of my Father in heaven not a hair can fall from my head; indeed, that all things must work together

for my salvation. Wherefore, by His Holy Spirit, He also assures me of eternal life, and makes me heartily willing and ready from now on to live for Him.[4]

God is my support – he never sleeps

In the rest of Psalm 121, the pilgrim applies the great truths articulated in the first stanza:

He will not let your foot slip –
 he who watches over you will not slumber;
indeed, he who watches over Israel
 will neither slumber nor sleep.
(Ps. 121:3–4)

Along the journey, there are places that are dark and difficult and where it is easy to slip and fall. The same is true in life. Suffering takes a variety of forms – physical, emotional, relational, financial and so on. The only condition for suffering is to live long enough.

Who is keeping watch? The psalmist lays his head on his pillow knowing that it is the Lord who watches over him. We think of this Psalm as our looking up to God, but it is actually about God watching over us. The phrase is repeated five times: 'he who watches over you will not slumber' (v. 3); 'he who watches over Israel' (v. 4); 'The LORD watches over you' (v. 5); 'he will watch over your life' (v. 7); 'the LORD will watch over your coming and going' (v. 8).

The Hebrew verb, translated as 'watch over', carries the idea of keeping guard, of showing care, of safety and security and shelter. Elsewhere it is used to refer to a watchtower. The pilgrim caravan would employ heavily armed bodyguards to protect it. The Lord is the bodyguard of his people. When the sleeper is troubled by disturbing dreams, he wakes for a moment and sees his bodyguard standing watch and he knows that all is well.

Human beings need sleep just as much as they need food and drink and oxygen. When we sleep, we are vulnerable. For all our foolish boasting, we are reminded every day that we are not invincible. But God never sleeps. He is always alert and always awake. He is the sleepless watchman who stands guard.

On 25 January 1736, John Wesley was crossing the Atlantic Ocean. Among the passengers with him, there was a group of German Moravian Brethren. He was deeply impressed by their piety and simple faith. He joined them for worship, but as they sang psalms, a terrible storm began. He wrote this in his journal:

> A terrible screaming began among the English. The Germans calmly sung on. I asked one of them afterwards, 'Was [*sic*] you not afraid?' He answered, 'I thank God, no.' I asked, 'But were not your women and children afraid?' He replied, mildly, 'No; our women and children are not afraid to die.'[5]

David captures this spirit of confident rest in God in Psalm 3:

> But you, LORD, are a shield around me,
>   my glory, the One who lifts my head high.
> I call out to the LORD,
>   and he answers me from his holy mountain.
> I lie down and sleep;
>   I wake again, because the LORD sustains me.
> I will not fear though tens of thousands
>   assail me on every side.
> (Ps. 3:3–6)

We can sleep because he never does! There is no point in us both staying awake!

God is my shade – he never leaves

In the next stanza, the psalmist builds on this confidence in God:

> The LORD watches over you –
>   the LORD is your shade at your right hand;

the sun will not harm you by day,
    nor the moon by night.
(Ps. 121:5–6)

Once again, he is clear about the perils we may face while on our journey. It is pretty obvious that the sun can harm us. If we do not find shade in a hot desert, we are in danger of sunstroke. If the core temperature of the body rises above 40 degrees centigrade, then our life is in danger. We may experience dehydration, a throbbing headache, confusion, disorientation, loss of consciousness and death.

But why do we need protection from the moon? Ancient peoples often associated the moon with madness or lunacy. A person can be 'moonstruck'. It may refer to this, or the writer may be alluding to the fact that we are at our most vulnerable at night. The pilgrim is afraid of what lies just beyond the comforting light of his campfire. During the night, molehills become mountains.

Taken together, this reminds us that we face perils on the journey both day and night. In other words, we cannot escape. Trials may harm us at any time of the day or night. The word 'harm' may be translated as 'smite' or 'beat' or 'strike'. Trials can be extremely painful and debilitating.

But in these circumstances, God stays close. The reference to the shade God provides is a reminder that he is near to us. We may not see him or feel his presence, but we are under his shadow. His shade is the place of protection from harm. It is also a reminder that he is close. You cannot give shade at a distance or cast a shadow from far off.

One Christmas, my son was admitted to hospital because of an asthma attack. It is terrifying for a little three-year-old to have to fight for every breath. The hospital staff set up a camp bed next to the bed where he lay being nebulized. My wife spent a sleepless night watching over him. Every time he woke, he saw her smile and heard her reassuring words of comfort. She was near.

And God is always close to his people. Listen to the words of Isaiah:

When you pass through the waters,
    I will be with you;
and when you pass through the rivers,
    they will not sweep over you.
When you walk through the fire,
    you will not be burned;
    the flames will not set you ablaze.
(Isa. 43:2)

God's people belong to him. He has created and shaped them; he has redeemed and summoned them. Therefore he can say, 'You are mine.' Because of this, every decision must be directed towards the one to whom we belong. It is his good pleasure, not ours, that counts. It also means that we are his responsibility. We are his treasured possession, and he will guard us and not let us go, even if we make unwise decisions.

Like the psalmist. God is realistic about the perils we face – raging waters, torrential rivers and blazing fires. But he promises his presence and protection. His shade will always overshadow us.

God is my Saviour – he never quits

In the final stanza, the psalmist celebrates the truth that God's watchful presence is permanent:

The LORD will keep you from all harm –
    he will watch over your life;
the LORD will watch over your coming and going
    both now and forevermore.
(Ps. 121:7–8)

Being kept from harm does not suggest an absence of all pain and heartache. We can still make mistakes and have to live with distressing consequences. He does not remove the problems, but he grips us with his grace. He does not take us out of the furnace, but he stands with us in the heart of the fire. He does not promise an easy passage, but he has promised a safe arrival.

Jesus stands with us in the decisions we make, no matter how disastrous they may appear to worldly wisdom or how potentially harmful they may seem to our lives. The promise is not necessarily one of physical deliverance. Joseph went to prison and Naboth and Stephen were stoned to death – all because they made decisions that honoured God (Gen. 39:6–20; 1 Kgs 21:1–16; Acts 7:51–60). Jesus calls us to go the way of the cross.

> If the world hates you, keep in mind that it hated me first. If you belonged to the world, it would love you as its own. As it is, you do not belong to the world, but I have chosen you out of the world. That is why the world hates you. Remember what I told you: 'A servant is not greater than his master.' If they persecuted me, they will persecute you also. If they obeyed my teaching, they will obey yours also. They will treat you this way because of my name, for they do not know the one who sent me. (John 15:18–21)

The Bible does not promise protection from pain, but it does promise that God will continue to watch over us for the rest of our lives until we arrive safely at the end of our journey. When we go off to work in the morning and when we come home at night, his watch never fails. He watches us now and for evermore.

I currently have eight grandchildren. I watch over them in prayer every morning. A day does not go by without my praying for them. I intend to keep praying for them for the rest of my life. But one day my days of prayer will be over. Who will watch over them then? The answer is that God never ceases to watch, and he promises to keep us to the end of our pilgrimage. We do not need to fear evil because his rod and staff guide us and he walks with us, even through the valley of the shadow of death (Ps. 23:4).

What is a Christian? It is not someone who is morally perfect or religiously orientated or spiritually perceptive. It is a man or woman who knows his or her own smallness and sinfulness and stupidity, but who, nonetheless is looking to Jesus. Christians have cast themselves into his arms. All their hope and dreams, all their decisions and resolutions are submitted to him, and their one desire is to please him.

It is in this spirit that we seek guidance. It is in this spirit that we make our decisions.

Questions

1 'There is something written into our DNA that causes us to reach out to God when we are in extremis.' Do you think that is true? How could this help us in sharing the gospel with people?

2 How does the fact that God is infinitely powerful and intimately personal help us to make wise decisions?

3 Look at the answer to the first question of the Heidelberg Catechism. How does this help us when we face difficult decisions?

4 Read Psalms 3 and 4. What do they teach us about God's protection and care?

5 'God's people belong to him. He has created and shaped them; he has redeemed and summoned them. Therefore he can say, "You are mine." We are in a covenant relationship.' How should this affect the way we live?

Conclusion
Pilgrims in this barren land

My wife's dad was the godliest man I have ever known. He was an elder in the church in which I was saved. When I married Edrie, I got to know him. I passed his bedroom at five o'clock one morning and, hearing a noise, I looked through the crack in the door and saw this octogenarian on his knees in passionate prayer. Shortly after that he was one of the key figures in planting a church near his home.

Dad took the F. B. Meyer view of guidance: 'The circumstances of our daily life are to us an infallible indication of God's will, when they concur with the inward promptings of the Spirit and the Word of God.'[1]

Whenever I asked his advice, it was always good advice; he would talk wisely about circumstances and inner peace and then ask, 'Has the Lord given you a verse?'

He was old school and expected God to speak to him in his daily devotions. By that he meant that he looked for a verse that seemed to give a clear direction. So if he was thinking of moving home he would anticipate a verse such as, 'Build houses and settle down' (Jer. 29:5).

I had to confess that I had never found this form of guidance particularly convincing, but it did not diminish my respect for him. His love for God meant that he would never have chosen a pathway that contradicted the plain teachings of Scripture.

I have reached the conclusion that, in his grace, God often accommodates himself to each person's individual personality and character traits. We can trust him all the way. He will never forsake those whom he has called. We may not be able to see the far horizons, but we can be assured of our ultimate destiny. With David we can sing:

> Surely your goodness and love will follow me
> > all the days of my life,
> and I will live in the house of the LORD
> > for ever.
> (Ps. 23:6)

The way may be difficult and it may be littered with deliberate sins or misjudgments and flawed decisions. But he will bring us home, and on the way we will come to know our Guide and lean on his unfailing faithfulness. He may lead us on a difficult pathway so that through a thousand intimacies with him the way may be forever memorable.

In the last hours of his life, Dad drifted in and out of consciousness. We gathered at his bed and, although we are not a particularly musical family, we sang to him. Dad's parents were saved in the Welsh Revival and he gloried in his Welsh roots. So we sang the great words of William Williams:

> Guide me, O my great Redeemer,
> pilgrim through this barren land;
> I am weak, but you are mighty;
> hold me with your powerful hand.
> Bread of heaven, bread of heaven,
> feed me now and evermore,
> feed me now and evermore.

> Open now the crystal fountain,
> where the healing waters flow.
> Let the fire and cloudy pillar
> lead me all my journey through.
> Strong Deliverer, strong Deliverer,
> ever be my strength and shield,
> ever be my strength and shield.

When I tread the verge of Jordan,
bid my anxious fears subside.
Death of death, and hell's Destruction,
land me safe on Canaan's side.
Songs of praises, songs of praises
I will ever sing to you,
I will ever sing to you.[2]

Dad had trusted his Guide through a long and fruitful life. He felt himself a pilgrim in a barren land and he knew his weaknesses. But he also knew the abundant provision of the Guide.

Dad had walked with his strong Deliverer and sensed his guiding hand as he led him to the streams of healing waters.

To the very end of his life, even as he trod the verge of Jordan, Dad trusted his Shepherd to lead him home.

His Shepherd did not fail him.

Notes

Introduction

1 Matt Perman, 'Was William Carey Being Biblical When He Said "Expect Great Things from God"?', 21 February 2011, <mattperman.com/2011/02/was-william-carey-being-biblical-when-he-said-expect-great-things-from-god>.
2 J. I. Packer, *Knowing God*, 3rd edition (London: Hodder & Stoughton, 2005), p. 31.
3 George Macdonald, *Annals of a Quiet Neighbourhood* (London: Wentworth Press, 2019), p. 206.

1 Clearing the decks

1 Steve Tamayo, 'Understanding & Growing in Wisdom', InterVarsity, 6 December 2019: <intervarsity.org/blog/understanding-growing-wisdom>.
2 Examples of God's revealed will or will of desire would be the Ten Commandments (Exod. 20:1–17) in the Old Testament or the Sermon on the Mount (Matt. 5:1 – 7:29) in the New Testament.
3 Gerald Sittser, *The Will of God as a Way of Life: Finding and Following the Will of God* (Grand Rapids: Zondervan, 2000), p. 17.
4 J. I. Packer, *Knowing God*, 3rd edition (London: Hodder & Stoughton, 2005), pp. 115–116.

2 Listening to God

1 'John Newton on Divine Guidance', in J. I. Packer and Carolyn Nystrom, *Guard Us, Guide Us: Divine Leading in Life's Decisions* (Grand Rapids: Baker, 2008), p. 246.
2 See Nigel Beynon and Andrew Sach, *Dig Deeper: Tools to Unearth the Bible's Treasure* (Wheaton: Crossway, 2010).
3 John Stott, *The Contemporary Christian* (London: IVP, 1992), p. 130.

4 Gerald Sittser, *The Will of God as a Way of Life: Finding and Following the Will of God* (Grand Rapids: Zondervan, 2000), p. 28.

3 Led by the Spirit

1 Lois Neely, *Come up to This Mountain* (Wheaton: Tyndale, 1980), p. 65.
2 Simon Browne, 'Come, gracious Spirit, heavenly Dove' (1720).
3 J. I. Packer, *Your Father Loves You: Daily Insights for Knowing God* (Wheaton: Harold Shaw Publishers, 1986), 1 February.
4 I have written about this experience in the book *Invest your Suffering: Unexpected Intimacy with a Loving God* (London: IVP, 2013).
5 John R. W. Stott, *The Message of Ephesians*, The Bible Speaks Today (London: IVP, 1984), p. 67.

4 Speaking to God

1 Quoted in Garry Friesen with J. Robin Maxson, *Decision Making and the Will of God* (Colorado Springs: Multnomah Press, 1980), p. 62.
2 Jonathan Edwards, *Basic Writings* (New York: New American Library, 1966), p. 142.

5 Finding wisdom

1 'June Daily Devotion: Week 4', The Billy Graham Library, 24 June 2018: <billygrahamlibrary.org/blog-june-daily-devotional-week-4>.
2 James C. Petty, *Step by Step: Divine Guidance for Ordinary Christians* (Phillipsburg: P and R Publishing, 1999), p. 144.
3 Proverbs 4:14–19; 12:26; 13:20; 14:7; 16:19; 18:24; 19:4, 6–7; 22:24–25; 29:3.
4 For example, www.simplyapreacher.com.

6 What about . . . ?

1 See chapter 8.
2 Acts 14:27; 1 Corinthians 16:8–9; 2 Corinthians 2:12–13; Colossians 4:3; Revelation 3:8.

3 R. T. Kendall, *Jonah: An Exposition* (London: Hodder & Stoughton, 1978), p. 29.

4 <philosiblog.com/2013/08/15>.

5 Gerald Sittser, *The Will of God as a Way of Life: Finding and Following the Will of God* (Grand Rapids: Zondervan, 2000), p. 28.

7 Putting it all together

1 From the hymn, 'Take my life', by Frances Ridley Havergal (1874).

2 D. Martyn Lloyd-Jones, *The Christian Warfare: An Exposition of Ephesians 6:10 to 13* (Edinburgh: Banner of Truth Trust, 1976), p. 114.

3 Kevin DeYoung, *Just Do Something: How to Make a Decision without Dreams, Visions, Fleeces, Open Doors, Random Bible Verses, Casting Lots, Liver Shivers, Writing in the Sky, etc* (Chicago: Moody Publishers, 2009).

4 Tim Challies, *The Discipline of Spiritual Discernment* (Wheaton: Crossway, 2007), p. 116.

8 Finding a spiritual home

1 Attributed to John C. Maxwell. Source unknown.

9 Work, rest and play

1 Mark Greene, *The Great Divide* (London: LICC, 2010), p. 4.

10 Tying the knot – or not

1 'Divorces in England and Wales: 2019', Office of National Statistics, 17 November 2020: <https://www.ons.gov.uk/peoplepopulationandcommunity/birthsdeathsandmarriages/divorce/bulletins/divorcesinenglandandwales/2019#:~:text=1.-,Main%20points,of%20completed%20divorces%20in%202019>.

2 From a sermon by Vaughan Roberts.

11 Knowing our Guide

1 James Paton (ed.), *John G. Paton, Missionary to the New Hebrides: An Autobiography* (Edinburgh: Banner of Truth, 1889, 1965), p. 56.

2 Paton (ed.), *John G. Paton*, p. 56.

3 Paton (ed.), *John G. Paton*, p. 79.

4 Paton (ed.), *John G. Paton*, p. 200.

5 Paton (ed.), *John G. Paton*, p. 200.

6 Packer, *Knowing God*, 3rd edition (London: Hodder & Stoughton, 2005), p. 31.

7 John Piper, 'Live for Your Greatest Desire', Desiring God, 23 February 2020: <www.desiringgod.org/messages/live-for-your-greatest-desire>.

8 Augustine, *The Confessions of St Augustine* (London: Penguin, 2002), p. 21.

12 Trusting our Guide

1 Tom Brokaw, *The Greatest Generation* (New York: Random House, 1998).

2 Sue Elliott and Steve Humphries, *Britain's Greatest Generation: How Our Parents and Grandparents Made the Twentieth Century* (London: Random House, 2015), p. xi.

3 See William Shakespeare, *Macbeth*, Act 5, scene 5, lines 19–28.

4 R. Scott Clark, 'What Is Your Only Comfort in Life and in Death?', The Heidelblog, 23 January 2021: <heidelblog.net/2021/01/what-is-your-only-comfort-in-life-and-in-death>.

5 Robert Booth, 'John Wesley with the Moravians in a Storm', <rwbooth.com/2016/01/25/john-wesley-with-the-moravians-in-a-storm>.

Conclusion

1 F. B. Meyer, *The Secret of Guidance* (New York: Fleming H. Revell Co., 1896), p. 16.

2 William Williams (1717–91), 'Guide me, O my great Redeemer'.